do you know how lucky you are?

PRAISE FOR *DO YOU KNOW HOW LUCKY YOU ARE?*

'A deeply felt exploration of daughterhood, migration, the loss and reclamation of language, and the perennial human story of finding solid ground amongst the wreckage of history. In spare, scintillating prose, Neutill tells the familiar story of immigrants in ways so startlingly new, it tests the very foundation of memoir itself, what it can do, who it is for, and how it breaks itself into something true.'

—Ocean Vuong

'Rani Neutill is a writer of passion and conviction. Her story is urgent. Read it.'

—Viet Thanh Nguyen

'Rarely does memoir so deftly combine beautiful writing with a profoundly important story. Neutill is a master in the making. Race, sexuality, class, religion, and so much more fit effortlessly into a mythical mother–daughter story. You'll never forget this book.'

—Garrard Conley

'A captivating debut that deftly explores the magic and chaos of an unforgettable mother–daughter relationship. With beautiful prose, Rani Neutill renders the burden of beauty, how women's bodies become a battleground, and the psychic costs of intergenerational trauma. Heart-wrenching and palpable in its yearning and love.'

—Marjan Kamali

do you know how lucky you are?

a mother–daughter memoir

rani neutill

HarperCollins *Publishers* India

First published in India by HarperCollins *Publishers* 2025
HarperCollins *Publishers* India, Cyber City,
Building 10-A, Gurugram, Haryana – 122002, India
www.harpercollins.co.in

2 4 6 8 10 9 7 5 3 1

P-ISBN: 978-93-7307-103-9
E-ISBN: 978-93-7307-556-3

Typeset in 11/15.2 Sabon LT Std
by HarperCollins *Publishers* India Pvt. Ltd

Printed and bound at
Replika Press Pvt. Ltd.

FSC
www.fsc.org
MIX
Paper | Supporting responsible forestry
FSC™ C016779

This book is produced from independently certified FSC® paper to ensure responsible forest management.

HarperCollins *Publishers*, Macken House, 39/40 Mayor Street Upper,
Dublin 1, D01 C9W8, Ireland

Disclaimer

The book is based on real events, recreated through first-hand accounts and narrated anecdotes. In instances, names have been changed, events compressed and dialogues recreated by the author for reliability.

This book is an autobiographical insight into the author's life, capturing her moments of trauma and how she deals with them. The content of this book should not replace consultation with your doctor or qualified mental health specialists for anyone experiencing anxiety, depression, suicidal ideation, or any other emotional or mental health concerns. The author and the publisher disclaim any liability or responsibility to any person or entity for any loss, damage, injury, or expense that may arise from the use of any content in this book. Any use of, or reliance on, information in this book is solely the responsibility of the reader.

For Will, who helped me tell this story
For my mother, who gave me this story to tell

'Because sometimes that is the only way to remember what is in your bones. You must peel off your skin, and that of your mother, and her mother. Until there is nothing. No scar, no skin, no flesh.'

—Amy Tan

'I believe I am writing about my mother because it is my turn to bring her into the world.'

—Annie Ernaux

WINTER 2015
ARRIVAL

I DON'T WANT TO SEE my mother. Returning to her is like running into a house on fire. Can I salvage the memories, the love, the connection we once had before the beams collapse and trap me?

I don't want to see my mother. Nonetheless, I have travelled forty-eight hours to save her.

As I exit the airport, the smoke of Kolkata engulfs my face, laces my lungs and stings my eyes. My tongue is chalky from lack of sleep, and I am confused about the date and time. I want to shower and rinse away the grime of travel and delay the moment when I see my mother. But I know I need to reach her as soon as possible.

A car arrives to drive me to my childhood home. Though it is 21 degrees centigrade outside, I shiver. In Kolkata, winters are warm and humid and crisp all at once, so different from where I live in Cambridge, Massachusetts, with its frigid, clear blue skies. In Kolkata, the sun is always obscured by the smoke from stacks of burning trash.

As we get closer to the city, I take in the new housing developments that have sprung up along the edges. These concrete high-rises didn't exist when I was younger. Only the chaiwallahs who sit by the side of the road, with roiling pots of cardamom tea, and hot coffee in huge, battered steel kettles that send pirouettes of steam into the air, remain. This, and the deftly choreographed dance of scooters, buses and cars outside my passenger window. I marvel at how the vehicles manoeuvre around each other, miraculously escaping collision, and the nearly indecipherable way they communicate via the *beep beep beep* of their horns. This is a sound I'd almost forgotten. A sound from a life I have fought to leave behind. A life with my mother.

Days before, I was lying in bed, cocooned in a down blanket, when the urgent summons that would compel me to travel to India arrived. My feet ached from a long day of waiting tables at a bar where MIT grad students mingled with biotech geniuses. As I scrolled, mesmerized, through a cascade of Facebook posts and wedding announcements, I reached out to pet my beloved chihuahua, Banjo, who was curled up in a bun beside me. A message from my cousin Niraj suddenly appeared on my laptop screen. I froze, photos of newborn babies and cute adopted dogs instantly forgotten. *You need to bring your mother back home.* My body stiffened and a knot of air gripped my throat as he explained that my mother's health was rapidly declining. Her mind was losing its purchase on reality. She urgently needed medical care.

More than a year had passed since I had last seen my mother. During that time, she had been living in Kolkata with her older sister, my aunt Rima, in the same flat I had lived in as a young girl without my mother. I called every month to check in on her, and every month Rima Mashi answered the phone.

'How is she?' I would ask.

'She is okay, okay. I am taking care,' Rima Mashi would quickly reply. She never handed the phone to my mother, and I never asked to speak to her. With each affirmation of my mother's well-being, I felt assuaged. But the feeling was ephemeral, just like the calm before a tornado. The winds die down and the air is still. Then, the sky mutates into a spire that cuts through the earth like the whirling blades of a blender.

Here was the tricky truth of it—I had left the work of my mother's physical care to my aunt because I hadn't wanted to be near my mother. I had fought for five years in court to be my mother's guardian, to wrest her back as her mind decayed. I needed to know that she was safe—but also at a safe distance. I didn't perform the role of the Indian daughter who takes her mother home and cares for her despite any conflict between them because I abhorred her touch. Because being near her madness reignited my own madness. Because I thought if I found myself in the same room with her, my mind might explode into bloody bits of confetti. I took refuge in the 12,000 kilometres between us, the boundless Atlantic Ocean protecting me from the cutlasses of her hands, the fury of her words.

So, when I received the message from Niraj, I didn't want to move. Still, an incomprehensible sliver of me felt drawn to safeguard my mother once again and to fight to be her guardian. Consciously, I wanted to force myself to never speak to her again, abandon her, and be done with her presence. But a tenacious reflex to protect her always prevailed because my relationship with my mother is a quantum entanglement—we are particles a universe apart, yet intimately linked and forever dependent upon each other.

I have been trying to understand my mother's madness and the rupture between us my entire life. It was this quest for answers that led me to pursue a doctorate in Ethnic Studies, reading stacks and stacks of books that detailed South Asia's complicated history. I enrolled in course after course in anthropology, literature and feminist theory. I tried to narrate the ways colonialism acted as a psychological condition, twisting and distorting the lives of my Dida—my mother's mother—and each of my aunts. I read about the effects of racism and sexism on the bodies and minds of women like my grandmother, aunts and mother. The history was so complex and dense that I could barely comprehend its detail and scope.

My studies enriched my life, but they couldn't give me what I most desired—an understanding that would allow me to forgive my mother her furies. Her refusal to seek help. Her abandonment. Nor, it turned out, could they provide me stability. I was told that a life of the mind would be a safe and prosperous path, but in the end, I wasn't able to find a full-time academic job. Instead, I had become an itinerant postdoctoral fellow, wandering from institution to institution. Now, I was a server at a bar. A grown woman trying to figure out what to do next.

During my time as an academic, I had journeyed through various elite institutions, always on some level seeking the approval of my mother. I wanted to prove to her that I was a good child who was smart and successful like the other Indian children I grew up with, kids to whom she always compared me. But whenever she saw me, she would say, 'You think you are smarter than me just because you taught at Harvard? You are not.'

This mess of repulsion and love for my mother compelled me to untangle myself from my warm blanket and wander into the living room, where Will, my husband of two months, sat on the couch working on his master's in computer science. Our terrier, Pancake, snuggled beside him, her scruffy golden head resting on his knee, the white tip of her tail on his thigh. I didn't want to disturb the serene life we had built together—the small, dishevelled apartment we lived in, with its one bedroom that overlooked the arterial Massachusetts Avenue; the three rescue pups that were our constant companions, the plush mattress we sank into after we made love each night, our newlywed joy.

'Will?'

He looked up at me, his light brown hair lit by the soft glow of the lamp beside him. I was standing in the doorway, my hands curled into tight fists to remind myself that I had to deal with my mother.

'My mom is sick. Niraj says I need to go get her. Should I?'

Will's posture is always impeccable—he does not hunch over as I do—but at my news, he sat up even taller. He knew I was about to go no matter how he answered.

'I can come with you,' he finally replied.

He wanted to help, to care for me as he always did. He viewed me as someone to love and protect—qualities I had never experienced as a child. But he had no place in my mother's world. I knew I had to go by myself.

When I arrive at Dida's building, I note that the soot staining the mustard-coloured exterior hasn't encroached or receded even a bit since my last visit. The building is a concrete archive of my family's history; the relationships inside have remained as static as the dirt on the walls. It houses the stories of my six aunts, my Dida, my mother and me. So many tragedies befell my family here. So much fighting transpired inside these walls. As I walk up the wide staircase, I hear the bustle of people inside each flat, the clang of stainless steel pots and pans, the sizzle of fish falling into hot oil. I grasp the large brass handle, shaped like a lion, and knock to announce my arrival. A moment passes, and then Rima Mashi unlocks the white door. She is a thin woman, and at my height her eyes meet mine head on.

'*Esho, esho,*' she says, gesturing me to enter.

She looks older than the last time I saw her. The teeth that remain are black and yellow from years of chewing paan, her gums barren and fleshy where there are gaps. For as long as I can remember, her smile has appeared decayed while the rest of Rima Mashi always looked incongruously young. She dyed her hair blue-black for years, and her face never showed a wrinkle. Now, she is seventy-five and I can see at once that she has become elderly. Crow's feet huddle around the corners of her eyes. Half-circles frame her mouth. Her hands shake.

Rima Mashi escorts me to my childhood bedroom. Inside, I find my mother sitting in a wooden chair. As a young woman, she had been fearsome, with a temper so explosive that everyone—no matter how much authority they wielded—seemed afraid of her. Now, she looks frail. I never thought she could appear so broken. Her legs are bent but splayed wide, a pose she might have once called 'unladylike'. She is dressed in a pink cardigan buttoned all the way up to her neck. The sweater seems as if it might be stifling her. She looks embalmed, her eyes dull like frosted glass, her mouth open in a perpetual *ahhh,* but she is too filthy to have passed through the hands of an undertaker. Her cheeks are streaked with dirt instead of blush. At the sight of me, her eyes widen in recognition, the corners of her mouth turn upwards. I can see that she is trying to raise her arms. She wants to stretch them towards me—to feel me, hug me, acknowledge that, *yes,* this is her daughter. But she doesn't reach for me. Instead, she pisses herself.

I watch, my own mouth agape, as Rima Mashi retrieves a towel from the armoire beside the bed and drops it on the floor. She uses her foot to mop up the mess, wiping the towel round and round, streaking the floor with swirls of urine. 'Can you imagine ... this is what happens to us?' she says.

My mother is sitting there, rivulets of urine trickling down the back of her legs. I am not yet capable of comprehending my mother's condition or the circumstances surrounding it. Staring at my mother as she inhabits this liminal space between life and death, this blur between reality and nothingness, only one thought passes through my mind—*this cannot be my mother.*

I remember what she used to look like, the way men stared at her, how their gazes remained fixed on her full bosom, then travelled across her unblemished skin, lingering on her bright brown eyes, night-black hair, thick eyebrows that arched like the twin roofs of an Art Deco masterpiece. Her plump pink lips must have looked sweet to them, like candy.

When I was young, I gazed at my mother in awe. Her face was perpetually lit up by a crescent of sunlight. Her teeth sparkled as bright as Venus. I wanted to be absorbed by her body as if she were quicksand. My love for her was infinite and immovable, the kind that can ruin you and strip you of your own identity. You are no one without the being you love. I clung to her leg and wailed when she needed to go somewhere without me. Pangs of longing and grief consumed me, as though her momentary absence meant I had lost her forever and I would never recover.

Now, my stomach bubbles. I have to look away from this version of my mother (as I have been doing for the last twenty years). I turn to the wall beside me. A photo of the young woman my mother once was hangs there. It's an enormous black-and-white photograph that my Dida took in the early 1960s. The photo flaunts that hypnotic glamour my mother once possessed. At seventeen, her hair is so black it looks like the expanse of a universe devoid of stars. Her eyes are outlined with thick kajol to draw attention to their shape and size. Her eyebrows are drawn in, their lines sharp and arresting. Four feet tall and three feet wide, the photograph is impossible to ignore, a presence in the room that looms over my mother, whose hair is now almost gone—what remains is white with a few threads of gold. Her eyebrows have faded away, too. Her eyes jaundiced. These two versions of my mother haunt the room—the beautiful woman she once was and the near-corpse she has become.

It doesn't occur to me until later that Rima Mashi has intentionally repositioned this photograph, moving it from elsewhere in the house, so that it lies within my mother's line of sight. At this moment, I don't question why she has done this, for all I feel is the kind of horror that tightens the skin, physically protecting it from an outside threat. The body responds to the mind, a tension that feels like it could freeze the blood and stop the heart.

Although my heart does not stop beating, it is breaking.

Before my arrival, I found a doctor who agreed to a house visit. Now, we wait for him. As I walk towards my mother, I notice she is slipping from the chair. There is no meat on her bones, no power in her to combat the pull of gravity. I step past the remnants of her urine and cup my hands beneath her armpits, lifting her to move her to the bed beside us. It's a bed that once held us both, and then me without her. I lay her down and take out a cotton bedcover from the armoire. As I walk back to her, my feet begin to slip—the urine on the floor has yet to dry and is as pungent as the hilsa and tangra sold in the Kolkata fish markets.

I place the blanket over her, covering her to the neck. Suddenly my disgust falls away and protective instincts in me take over. My mother's brokenness allows me to recover the rabid love I had for her during my youngest years. In her state of frailty, she cannot yell at me. She cannot hurt me. She is no longer a threat, and I feel an overwhelming need to care for her.

It's my duty as her daughter. But first I need to steel myself. I need to section off the part of me where grief and the pain of loss are stored so I can save her.

'Are you cold?' I ask.

She doesn't reply.

I desperately need someone to tell me what is wrong, to get my mother help.

When the doctor finally arrives, he performs his duties, taking her temperature and pulse, examining her body. He says my mother is malnourished. He is alarmed by how thin she is. Her bones are protruding from her skin. Her waist is so small that both my hands could encompass its width. She is wheezing, needs oxygen and probably has a urinary tract infection. A sharp odour in the air mixes with the ammonia of my mother's urine. The smell makes me vaguely aware something terrible is happening to her body.

The doctor says, 'We must rush her to the hospital.'

'Is she dying?' I ask.

'We will take care of her,' he replies.

The ambulance arrives. As its drivers work to shift my mother onto a tattered sheet, her face begins to cave in and her lips droop. The numbness I feel dissolves into panic. I think my mother is having a stroke. 'What is happening?' I ask.

'Her dentures. They are coming out,' Rima Mashi explains.

I have forgotten that twelve years ago, my mother went to a dentist for dentures, even though she didn't need them. She believed the aluminium fillings in her teeth were bad for her health and were giving her Alzheimer's. She was so vehement in her conviction that she let a dentist pull out each of her thirty-two perfectly healthy white teeth. Now, I pull the corrugated resin, gooey from her saliva, from between her lips. Her spit smears my fingertips as her mouth becomes concave. She is unrecognizable. This must be what she will look like when she dies, as shrivelled as a mummy, as frightening as a witch. I gently slide the dentures back in. I long to weep, but I can't let my mother know that I am horrified by how she looks. If my mother were able to see herself, she would be distressed to appear so unsightly. I forget, just for a moment, how many times my mother had commented on my appearance—either I was too fat or too thin; my skin was not as fair and flawless as hers. Instead, it was darker and plagued with acne. Now her skin is still light and unblemished, but it is yellow.

We gently guide my mother's body down the burgundy stairs, dimly lit by a single bulb precariously hanging from a broken socket. Outside my Dida's building, the city is bustling and the streetlights blaze. The medics shift my mother onto a small gurney and push her inside a tiny ambulance the size of a VW bus. I jump onto a plank of wood beside an old, rusty oxygen tank. We speed through the congested, pothole-ridden streets. Our bodies knock about in an uneven rhythm, the ambulance's siren sharp in our ears. The siren eclipses all the *beep, beep, beeping* of the cars in this city that always feels like home. I look down at my mother, and she looks up at me. I stroke her hair, gently braiding my hand with hers.

'Ma, I'm so sorry,' I whisper, as involuntary tears stream down my face.

On this day, my tears do not enrage her. She tries to touch my cheek with a quivering hand as if to say that it's okay, I shouldn't cry. But she doesn't have the voice to tell me what I most want to hear—that she forgives me.

1

MY MOTHER HAD MANY SUPERSTITIONS and believed owls were good luck. At night, if she heard a glimmer of a hoot, she would jump out of bed and run to the closet where we kept our earthquake supplies, a staple in Southern California—candles, water, flashlights, batteries, canned food, some tattered clothes and a few blankets. She would grab a large flashlight, and we would run outside, where she would aim the light towards the sky and through the trees to search for the shadowy outline of ruffled feathers perched on an electrical wire.

'You see that!' she said to me once, her arm outstretched as she shone a light on a white owl, its claws clutching the branch of a pine tree above us. 'That is good fortune!'

It was 3 a.m. 'Yes, Mama, I see!' I squealed, as I gazed up at the owl to take in its blessing. I imagined our good luck—sparkly gold glitter that shot from the owl's amber eyes to cover my skin with its grace.

'We are going to be okay, sona, I know it!' My mother's face was beaming as she smiled wide with glee, her teeth as bright as the owl's feathers. I smiled, too.

My mother's euphoria was exhilarating, her periods of joy infectious. The touch of her hand, her laughter, could be as thrilling as a ride down a rollercoaster. I basked in her conviction that our future was something wonderful to look forward to.

There were so many glorious moments with my mother. She would drive us for hours across California, Arizona and Nevada, blasting Bollywood soundtracks on the eight-tracks she had brought home from India. We'd drive towards Las Vegas and watch the dazzling lights of the city grow each year. We'd visit the Grand Canyon to take in its grandeur, and we'd marvel at the depth of the Hoover Dam. We'd sit side by side, holding hands, observing gutsy squirrels running up to tourists for food.

She loved to dance and spin me around our living room to the music of *Sholay* and *Bobby* as Lata Mangeshkar's silky voice glided through the air. These moments were filled with glee. When she was happy, the air crackled with excitement.

My mother and I shared the same bed until I was eleven. We slept in fits and starts, our home large and empty. She was always scared someone might invade our space, rob us, rape us. She suffered the isolation of a woman responsible for a girl-child, one of the most vulnerable of sexes; so, I was scared, too.

One day, when I had just turned eight, a skinny white woman rang our doorbell, and my mother opened our large wooden door. 'Hi, I'm part of a city committee that is raising awareness about safety precautions. Are you aware that there is a serial killer at large?' she asked.

My mother looked at the woman, her expression blank. We hadn't been watching the news.

She told us about Richard Ramirez, the Night Stalker, and his victims. How he walked into people's homes and shot them in the face. She said he had no fear. He killed people of all ages.

He bludgeoned, decapitated, butchered, stabbed and mutilated his victims.

We began to watch the nightly news. Waves of tension kept us up each night. I held my mother's hand as we lay awake on her bed, our eyes open, our minds buzzing. We were two females. The perfect prey.

Once, the sliding transparent doors that lined the back of our home had made it feel spacious, freeing. Now I saw them as gateways inviting our future murderer. I hated all that glass and was too scared to look into all the terrors the darkness hid; sometimes, I imagined serial killers monitoring everything we said and did. My mother and I took every precaution necessary, checking to see if all the doors and windows were locked. We repeated this ritual throughout the night, my mother unlocking and relocking hasps, tugging at the metal door handles to ensure the doors wouldn't slide open.

We heard on the news one day that Ramirez had stolen a white car. His murders, it seemed, were now occurring almost every night. We went to bed on high alert. Around midnight, the phone rang. Both of us jumped out of bed as my mother reached over to answer it.

'Hello?'

We shared the line ear-to-ear, the phone squished uncomfortably between our cheeks. We pressed our weight onto the receiver as if we were trying to extend ourselves into the telephone to find out who was calling. We waited for someone to answer. We heard nothing but deep, deliberate breaths.

'Hello?' my mother repeated.

The breathing grew heavier.

One more time. 'Hello?'

Nothing.

As my mother hung up, a car drove by. I felt all the hairs on my body stand up. Goosebumps prickled my arms. We rushed to the kitchen to peer out of the window. My mother crouched down. I held myself to the right of the glass—only my left eye peeked out. A white car was driving up and down our cul-de-sac. Back and forth, back and forth. The car seemed to make these laps slowly, as if the driver were scanning the neighbourhood. The car must have driven to and fro five or six times.

I knew it was the Night Stalker. He was driving in search of his next victims. For a moment, I was frozen. Then a deliberate sense of urgency took hold of me. I walked towards the phone on the kitchen wall, my arms outstretched as I moved one foot in front of the other, slowly, ready to pick it up and call 911. My mother was curled up under the window, her body a tight fist while she waited for me to dial the numbers. As the white car continued its laps up and down our street, time severed itself from any moving clock. I heard things in short increments, as if his car were driving only a quarter mile an hour and my feet were moving across the floor as sluggishly as two snails. Fear was the slime I left behind. I held my breath. Eventually, he drove away. I went to my mother and reached out for her hand. She coiled her fingers into mine as she rose off the ground. We were shaking.

All night, my mother listened for the sound of someone cracking open a window or stepping on a twig. The whites of her eyes were like moonlit snow, glistening with terror. When dawn came and sheets of light cut through the gap between our drapes, she shut her eyes and finally fell asleep.

There were other nights that kept us up as well, nights when the Santa Ana winds roared with fury. Those nights always followed the same pattern.

A large, three-paned window provided a view of our cul-de-sac. One day, when the winds were roaring, I stared out into the darkness of our neighbourhood, at the shadows of palm trees swaying. Their leaves looked like the weeping feathers of a wet bird. Wind whistled through the cracks in the windows and doors and warned us of its strength. Fear overtook my mother's body.

'Cholo, let's go,' my mother said.

I picked up my favourite toy, a worn-out stuffed animal that looked like Snoopy, and shoved it under my arm, its once-smooth surface now pilled and faded. She collected some of our belongings—clothes, numerology books, a statue of Ganesh, holy beads and a single stack of cash—and shoved them into our suitcase, a small forest-green bag with a bright line of red duct tape across it so we could easily identify it on any baggage carousel.

We drove to the nearest Motel 6. My mother panicked that we might lose everything except the small suitcase with a little bit of money and books meant to predict our future. The texts were her lifeline to security. My oldest aunt, Boro Mashi, had referred my mother to an astrologer who gave her the books and told her the days that were safe to travel.

'This is all we need,' she said. 'Sona, if god says we will be safe, we will be safe.'

Even in the motel room, my mother did not sleep. I stroked her hair, thinking it might ease her racing mind. She still couldn't sleep, so neither did I. In the morning, an eerie calm fell across Los Angeles County. The world hadn't been burnt away, and we had survived.

When I was five, six and seven years old, these visits to Motel 6 were cyclical, in line with the arrival of the relentless winds each year.

In the moments of panic, I wanted my mother to shield me from the horror of our house in a storm or a madman on the loose. I wanted her to be Superwoman. But she wasn't a superhero, and we were all alone. We had no relatives to call us or check in each day to see if we were still alive, no close community of friends or neighbours. She didn't have some innate ability to protect me, because she also needed protecting, and there was no one to protect her but me.

Occasionally, my mother found peace in astrological games. Many nights at 2 a.m., I sat on the floor of our long hallway and watched as she threw dice and consulted her Chinese numerology texts, her long hair brushing the Spanish tiles. She added up the dots and shuffled through the pages of her books to find answers to questions about our future, her lips moving as she ingested sentences, her mind fluttering in search of serenity. Those nights, like most, she sought the elusive knowledge of things to come. And because she searched for the answers to our future, I did as well.

I also searched for answers about our past.

In 1979, my white father died of pancreatic cancer, six days before my second birthday. After my father died, my life was solely my mother. We were one.

My parents had met through the mail. My mother had been working for the Indian Consulate in Germany and was visiting Delhi for Independence Day. There, she was introduced to an American man, my father's colleague. They took a photograph together and kept in touch. When my father saw the picture, he was entranced. My mother's round face and almond eyes—features that illustrated her distinct ethnicity—bewitched him.

He had been pursuing his doctorate in psychology through a correspondence programme and had become fascinated with Carl Jung and archetypes. He had read Jung's writings on Eastern religions and had grown intoxicated by Buddhism and Hinduism and its deities—Kali, the goddess of destruction; Ganesh, the remover of obstacles.

He asked for my mother's address from his colleague and wrote to her from Pasadena, California on a baby blue aerogramme with navy-blue and red stripes along the edges. He told her he wanted to visit India and asked her to teach him about all the inscrutable customs that made her nation so mesmerizing. My mother wrote back. They exchanged pictures of each other, flaunting their features—photos in which they smiled at the camera, each inviting the other in. They sent cassette tapes so that they could hear each other's voices, their inflections conveying emotion and intent.

My mother was twenty-nine. My father was over fifty. He flew my mother to Pasadena to be with him and bought her a house tucked neatly into the San Gabriel mountains, in a picturesque part of the city where gardens bloomed, lemons fell from trees and deer wandered across backyards, eating roses. The sky was filled with smog, the air dry—not humid like Kolkata, where my mother had been born and raised.

In my younger years, my mother relayed the story of how she and my father met. She had hoped for a better future, filled with the safety provided by a man who would love her and give her a big, bright home with the sound of children. Jewels on her dainty fingers. Financial security. She had told me that my father was a good man and that he loved me.

We were on her king-size bed as she pulled out photo albums that contained pictures of him. In the first photos, he was young and handsome, his shoulders broad, his complexion smooth and buttery. Not withered like the creased skin of a chicken, which is what he would eventually look like as he neared his death. She smiled as she told me how I was conceived on the thirteenth floor of a hotel room in Honolulu, how very romantic their lovemaking was, how she just knew a baby was going to come from their union that evening. She also told me that she wished I was born a boy. Boys faced fewer burdens in life. Boys could not get pregnant before marriage.

I remember little about my father, but his tapes lived next to the old vinyl Beatles albums and Bollywood soundtracks tucked inside the media console in our television room. The tapes were a confluence of my parents' sonic lives. They detailed my father's desire to meet my mother, touch her, envelop her. They had me mesmerized. I wanted to hear about my parents' union, not the story of my father's death. I wanted enchantment, not melancholy.

When I was four, five and six years old, I would insert a cassette into the tape deck, press play and lean against our tall speaker, my ear on the mesh grille. I'd absorb my father's voice and try to imagine him in the room with me—as a handsome young man, not as the old, cancer-ridden one who defecated in a bucket. I'd picture his hand running through my hair; his eyes filled with adoration. My body would warm up, as if his words were his touch. My hands would grip the speaker. My eyes would close, the vision of my father *there*, in the curtained space behind my eyelids. I'd feel at peace with each note of his voice, gratified by his archived existence.

When my mother found me one day, my ear to the mesh grille, my eyes fixed on the illusion of the father I had designed for myself, she yelled, 'You think losing your father is the worst thing! I grew up with nothing! No dolls like you have! You have *me*!' As I cowered, she grabbed the box of tapes from my hands and shoved them back into the media console.

When I recall my father now, I wonder at his intentions, even as I question my mother's submission to his desire for an Indian wife who was half his age. He was a white man from America attracted to a woman from far, far away. A woman with light brown skin and the blackest hair. A woman whose first language was not English. I know his erotic drives were rooted not only in this difference, but in her loveliness and youth and the idea that she would be a good and obedient wife.

I wonder—how might their marriage have worked out if he hadn't died? What kind of father would he have been—this man who married a woman because of her beauty and race?

As a child—let me admit it—I didn't think about my father's flaws. I just wondered what life might have been like with a man who could have taken care of my mother.

Then again, everyone seemed to understand my mother would not be taken care of. She was like Santa Ana's devil winds, untameable. No one could possess her—not even me.

2

MY MOTHER RAN THROUGH THE Mumbai airport with a mad sense of urgency.

'Do you have any flights to Madurai?' she asked the attendant at each airline counter. Madurai was the nearest airport to Kodaikanal, where her guru Sathya Sai Baba resided. Around 1,400 kilometres separated us from his benedictions and the salvation my mother believed he could offer; there were no flights to Madurai.

But we had to reach him. My mother would stop at nothing. Her next plan was to find a taxi. She dragged me along as she approached taxi after taxi outside the airport and peered into each car to assess the driver. She wanted to confirm he was someone she could trust, someone who would not rape or rob us. She found a taxiwallah, a kind old man dressed in a tattered lungi. Inside his car, he warned us of bandits who kidnapped women during the night and stole from tourists. A long, clean machete sat next to him as he drove, glinting in the sun. I was seven years old.

I curled my body in the backseat, but I didn't fall asleep during that entire twenty-four hour car ride. Instead, I watched the scenery of India pass us by as we drove north to south. Every hour, I would carefully raise my face to the window and observe all the lorries that drove past us. I wondered if they were filled with men who might mutilate us with their long knives. I somehow knew that rape meant the violation of a woman's body. I imagined men taking my mother somewhere into the jungle and irrevocably harming her. I shook with terror.

My skin felt like it was melting into the tattered vinyl of the seat, my sweat mixing with the heavy air. I watched people in autorickshaws, men on scooters, the way all the cars and trucks kicked up dirt and formed a never-ending cloud of dust. It was so different from Pasadena. The roads there were wide and evenly paved, and the white and yellow lines clearly demarcated where the sleek sedans and beat-up Camaros belonged. In California, there were no lorries painted blue, red and yellow, no automobiles recklessly weaving around one another, no trails of smoke and dust illustrating in which direction each car was headed, as though writing the story of their vehicular lives.

Every year, we made a pilgrimage to see Sathya Sai Baba, but this particular trip was frenetic. While we were in Mumbai, an astrologer had told my mother that it was an auspicious time and we needed to travel to Kodaikanal immediately, otherwise our fortune might shift. My mother believed wholeheartedly that our devotion to Sathya Sai Baba would at long last be rewarded and he would bless us. He would welcome us into his grand home, answer her burning questions about life and the universe, and grant her wishes.

If only we could reach him in time.

It was this steadfast belief that fuelled our frantic trip down the subcontinent of India.

Once again, two females, alone.

After my father died, my mother used the inheritance he left us to wander the world. I was her constant travel companion from the age of two. We visited India to see my Dida each year and hopped around Asia. My mother loved the constant movement of planes and trains, autorickshaws and taxis. I recall long, tiring plane rides on Singapore Airlines. She always requested the row with no seats in front, just a plastic wall and TV screen. We slept on the floor nuzzled together, wrapped in airline blankets, tiny pillows framing our heads—me, the baby spoon who fit perfectly into the crevices of her body as she held me tightly. I desperately desired these moments when her attention was fixed only on me. Between movement and transit were times for intimacy. Her wanderlust would be satisfied with travel to a temporary destination, and there'd be a pause in her discontent.

When I was five years old, my mother became obsessed with Sathya Sai Baba, a philanthropist who said he was a reincarnation of Sai Baba of Shirdi. The original Sai Baba was a saint who drew in followers of Hindu and Muslim faith by combining the teachings of both religions—a sort of peacekeeper in a nation that would become increasingly polarized. Sai Baba of Shirdi lived without worldly possessions, a true fakir.

Though millions of people from around the world were drawn to Sathya Sai Baba, my mother among them, he did not live like his namesake. Where Sai Baba of Shirdi was unconcerned with appearances, Sathya Sai Baba always wore a sumptuous, full-sleeved orange kurta that shimmered with cleanliness. His presence was unmistakable. He had homes in both Puttaparthi and the hillside tourist destination of Kodaikanal. His houses and cars were gifts from his many wealthy—and notably white—admirers in Western Europe and the United States.

Each of our visits to his home unfolded in the same fashion. First, Sathya Sai Baba would separate his followers by gender, with women and children huddled together away from the men. My mother and I would walk into the enclosure that surrounded his mansion and sit down. The hard earth beneath us always bestowed a sense of stability that dissipated as soon as Sai Baba arrived. Then, our bodies would tense with anticipation. I remember desperately wanting to see his bare feet approach us, to feel the stroke of his hand on my hair and receive his good tidings. My mother would raise her hands in prayer, and I'd mimic her movements, lifting my hands in worship. We'd wait for his acknowledgement. And wait and wait.

He'd walk around and wave, his pristine kurta trailing through the dust and dirt. My mother always held a note in her hand, hoping he would take it; her fears and desires as a single Indian mother scribbled onto small bits of paper.

Please keep us financially stable.
Please let Rani get a good education and find a husband.
When will I die?

Sai Baba would randomly choose devotees to bring into his mammoth house, where he was said to perform small miracles. He'd pluck fancy goods, like diamonds, emeralds and rubies out of thin air. Vibuthi—holy ash—would wondrously spring from his palms.

I never understood how he conjured these riches. I supposed he was performing a sleight-of-hand. He had yet to choose us, but my mother believed that this time would be different like the astrologer had told her. It was finally going to be our turn.

A white couple was walking towards us.

We had finally arrived at our hotel, remarkably unharmed after our 1,400 km drive down the subcontinent. When the couple reached the lobby where we were checking in, they approached us and asked if we were there to see Sai Baba. The woman held a little baby girl who couldn't have been more than five months old. I saw a large emerald ring encrusted with tiny diamonds on the woman's index finger. My mother looked at the ring, and the woman looked at her. The woman's blue eyes were piercing, my mother's dark brown eyes combusting with desire. The woman seemed to know that the expression on my mother's face was really a question.

'Oh, this? Yes, Sai Baba made this for me.' The woman explained that they lived in Beverly Hills. She had travelled from Los Angeles, just like us. She told us that Sai Baba had brought them into his home and performed his small miracles. Objects miraculously appeared—an emerald ring and a tiny figurine of some god. She pulled the statue from her purse, and we marvelled at it. I held the idol in my palm and imagined it was a medallion worn by a superhero, that by holding it I would be granted special powers. The woman told us that her family had been chosen, that they had bought Sai Baba a car in return for his blessings. There was a hint of superiority in her voice when she narrated this story, glancing at my mother with what I can only describe now as pity.

Sai Baba was known for using the money his wealthy devotees donated to build hospitals and schools in India for the poor. An educated, elite class of doctors and teachers offered their services to him in exchange for his blessings. I later learned that we did not have the money to give to his charities; whatever we had was rationed for travel, and my mother carefully budgeted her funds for each trip.

In our hotel room, my mother fiddled with our belongings, searching for some paper and a pen to write down all the questions she had for Sai Baba. I was exhausted, cold and very hungry. A big bed called out to me to lie down. I begged for room service. My mother ordered me my favourite meal—masala dosa—which arrived on a stainless steel thali with steam twisting through the air. The smell of potatoes and onions mixed with curry leaves, mustard seeds and green chillies, all wrapped in a long crêpe, overwhelmed me.

I stuffed my face, dropping pieces of the dosa into the coconut chutney and sambhar it was served with. Soon after, I began to throw up, heaving the food I had just devoured into the hotel toilet. I lay on the floor, peered up at the ceiling and wondered if my mother would find the answers she had come for.

The next morning, my mother pulled my shivering body up a hill, all 5 kilometres to Sai Baba's home.

'We must see him today,' she said. 'Today is the day. I know it.'

I tugged the edges of my woollen shawl tighter around me. I was weak, dizzy and dehydrated from the night before. But my mother's unquiet mind took over. I felt her desperate plea for answers, her belief she was nearing an opportunity. Her hair stretched back into a messy bun, wisps of it defining her round face. Her eyes were a panorama of hope and wonder.

I gazed at the endless path before me. A canopy of lush, emerald green trees marked the horizon. Suddenly, a thick fog surrounded us. I reached out to capture a handful of the tiny droplets that waltzed through the air. They disintegrated.

As I gathered my breath to continue, my mother grabbed my wrist.

'I'm trying, Mama. I'm trying,' I said. I knew I had to follow her. There could be no childish resistance. She was the only thing I had. I was in love with her, attached to her mind and body, and I only wanted to please her.

I shuffled forward.

'Mama, can we take a taxi? I don't feel good.'

'Na, sona, the fresh air will be good for you,' my mother declared, perhaps to convince herself that my illness would be cured by the journey to see Sai Baba and the consecration he would grant us. She thought if we walked those 5 kilometres, we would finally secure the benediction that she so vehemently believed Sai Baba was waiting to provide.

'We must walk. We must live minimally; the way Sai Baba has advised us.'

I didn't understand but trusted that my mother knew best. I believed her when she said that Sai Baba would bless us and keep us safe. I thought he would answer my mother's questions. He would make sure that we had money, that I would find a nice husband when I got older and that we would be safe from the perils of the outside world.

As we walked, I felt dizzier and dizzier from the elevation. I paused to regain my balance and tensed my legs to make them strong enough to carry me. A shiny white Ambassador approached us and slowed its pace. Inside, I saw the American couple and their baby. The wife turned to look at us and my gaze met hers, lingering on her face and that of her child. They both looked so healthy and happy. Suddenly, I felt sick again. I bent over and vomited onto the dusty ground. As I did, the car drove past us towards Sai Baba's compound.

I now know that my mother's fierce desires were treacherous. That the blind need to find answers was dangerous. Later, her tendency to follow the men she believed were prophets would imperil her life. But at seven, I just noted the difference in race between my mother and me, and the couple in the immaculate car. I wondered why Sai Baba had chosen them and had not yet chosen us. Mostly I felt confused—how could the couple, ardent devotees, leave a small girl and her mother behind—that too, a sick child who should not have been walking kilometres to see a man who represented an almighty force. I suddenly understood the meaning of hypocrisy, even if I did not possess that word.

When we finally reached Sai Baba's home, hundreds of people were entering the arched columns of his compound. A chorus of men played tablas and carried Sai Baba in on a velvet throne. He was placed directly before us and raised his hands, his palms facing us. Eventually, he climbed off his regal chair and walked around, pointing at those worshippers he wanted to bring into his house. I felt dizzier than ever. Sweat trickled from my armpits and trailed down my torso, but I was still cold.

Sai Baba asked the white woman with her baby to rise and join the chosen few. My mother looked at her with hunger, hoping the astrologer's predictions would come to fruition and Sai Baba would gesture for us to join the woman so we could rejoice. He didn't pick us.

He never would.

The trip to see Sai Baba was just one of many around-the-world excursions.

My mother believed our travels were an education, our life of pilgrimage, a curriculum of lessons in worldliness and spirituality. To her, voyages were better than traditional schooling and our trips often extended past the dates of my school's reopening. As a result, my academic years felt fragmented.

'Do you know how lucky you are to have seen the world?' my mother liked to say whenever I complained about being tired or ill.

I was lucky. My mother provided me with a schooling of global proportions. I assimilated these experiences as if they were ordinary—her pull of my hand as we walked miles to visit holy men, our globetrotting, her desire that I love her and no one else, which was fine, at that time, because nothing felt easier in the world than loving her. Our trips were magic and chaos all at once, and I normalized the constant journeying. I even revelled in it—the jagged, towering skylines of Hong Kong, the pungent smell of durian in Singapore, and the sun that peacefully descended on the Bali Sea. When we'd return to Pasadena, we'd resume our life together, a life that would contract to just the two of us. And for a little while, despite the anxiety and constant toing and froing, it felt like an ideal and extraordinary existence.

3

AFTER OUR PILGRIMAGE TO SAI Baba, we travelled to Kolkata to visit one of my aunts, Tapati Mashi, in the asylum where she was kept. There was barely any light as we walked through the damp hallways, where we were greeted by the stench of rotting wood. I covered my ears against a barrage of babbling, screaming and crying.

We found my Tapati Mashi sitting on the ground in a small room that could have been a jail cell, with concrete walls, a tiny bed and an even tinier window that let in a fragment of stale sunlight. My aunt's sari was tattered from days of wearing it. The fall had come apart at the seams; squiggly threads writhed like worms every time she moved. The sari had once been white—the colour that widows were told to wear. I had only ever seen my Dida in white. Tapati Mashi's sari was now the colour of oatmeal.

The room had a sink with a translucent red bucket underneath. I wondered if she bathed in the dark space of that room, how often she changed her clothes and who cared for her—for on that day, I saw no one at all. She seemed shrouded from the living, banned from society.

I was freshly bathed. My skin smelled like sandalwood soap, and I was dressed in one of my mother's old salwar kameezes. It was too big for me and obscured my body like a sheet on Halloween. I faded away, a silent observer, and watched my mother, as I so often did.

Tapati Mashi was a decade older than my mother. I did not recognize that she had once been striking. Only later did I see photographs of her, images in which she appeared untouched by the forces of madness. In those pictures, she was almost as alluring as my mother. Dressed in a magenta silk sari that enhanced her bronze complexion, she seemed acutely aware of her surroundings. Her flawless skin radiated good health and her sparkling eyes seemed fixed on the camera. That day in the asylum, I raised my gaze to meet her milky stare—these eyes did not see me. She laughed hysterically without reason.

My mother tried to hold my Tapati Mashi's hand and spoke to her in Bengali. '*Kemon acho*, how are you?' she asked, as she searched her sister's face for a look of recognition.

Tapati Mashi smiled a toothless grin, her mouth as vacant as her eyes. I wanted to look away from her. She was every child's worst nightmare—a zombie, an alien there to snatch me away. She was a witch who might condemn me to a fate like her own.

My mother jerked her arm away as Tapati Mashi cackled, as if her skin might become infected with the germs of insanity. She stuttered, unable to speak and say, *It's me, your sister, I love you*. Instead, my mother began to tremble. Her skin pulsed and her eyes fluttered about, searching her surroundings as if she were trying to make sure that she knew what was real and what was not. I could tell that my mother was petrified that she would suffer the same fate as her sister; she would be locked away forever, living amongst the forgotten.

When we left, I felt traces of my Tapati Mashi lingering behind. Even at seven, I understood that she represented something much bigger within my family, something that loomed, a reminder of a stained past and a future in which we were all in danger of stumbling into.

The next time my mother went to visit my aunt, I begged her to leave me behind. It is the only moment I can recall from my youngest years when I didn't want to follow my mother.

My mother loved to narrate the details of her birth, her childhood, stories about her siblings and their lives.

My mother was the second youngest of eight—seven girls and one boy. All of my mashis were colourful, each with a unique tale, each in some way tragic, with rumours of suicide, divorce, domestic abuse, widowhood or insanity marking their life stories. Even though their lives were mournful, I believed that my Dida and aunts were powerful. There were no men present in my family—my one uncle was rarely around during my childhood. There were no patriarchs to tell my Dida and mother what to do. Later, I'd realize that men defined how women lived and died, whether or not they were present. But back then, as far as I could tell, men were non-existent.

Though my mother loved to wander all over the world, it was Kolkata (back then, Calcutta) that she loved the most. She was born in the city in 1947, the same year as India's independence. It was impossible for her not to feel pangs of Bengali pride; Kolkata's role in the nation's struggle for freedom was pivotal. Resistance against the British was (arguably) born there, which became the capital of British India in 1772. As a century of colonial rule went by, the city grew to be the epicentre of the nationalist movement. Bengali writers like Rabindranath Tagore, Aurobindo Ghosh and Bankim Chandra Chatterjee—all writers my mother would have known of and read—flourished in Kolkata as thinkers, poets and activists whose writings carried a call for freedom. To stop the growing tension, colonial powers relocated their capital to New Delhi in 1911. Calcutta continued to fight back through poetry and prose. Revolutionaries sat at addas, drinking coffee in small clay cups, smoking bidis and plotting their way to liberation.

Even while resisting British rule, the city and its people were psychologically influenced by their colonizers. India gained freedom, but in Calcutta, traces of colonialism lingered everywhere, particularly in people's minds. The abuser always leaves an imprint on the abused.

The impact of colonialism was exceedingly clear when it came to my Dida. She was an unabashed Anglophile. Independence, to her, did not feel like liberation at all. When I was five, she told me that Indians were better off under British rule. '*Puropori porishkar*. Absolutely spotless!' she exclaimed, her eyes twinkling with the memory of a clean and colonized city. In my Dida's stories, the polluted lanes of Kolkata, under the British, transformed into avenues filled with shiny vehicles and women in fascinators. The streets sparkled. It was when the British left that the dust and dirt of the city arrived.

While my Dida despised a free Kolkata, I came to love the city's streets for what they offered—for the street dogs, and for men who travelled around with spider monkeys that wore hats and vests and stopped to perform for eager crowds. For me, Kolkata was meant to be a boisterous city full of delights.

My Dida couldn't understand me. She also didn't notice that the admiration she felt for the British wasn't mutual, that the British themselves believed her to be inferior, a primeval native of a nation they had dominated for 200 years.

As I grew older my Dida's tales about India's history became violent. She told me of Partition; of an independence that left bloody marks; of a butchering of the land and its people; of the worst kind of mob bloodshed. People who had been neighbours, friends and confidants, turned against each other in a flash of frenzy. They stabbed, mutilated and decapitated one another like a swarm of Night Stalkers.

Countless women were raped during the Partition, their bodies strewn across streets, invaded and disembowelled; unborn babies were ripped out of their amniotic homes. My Dida told me she hid on the roof of her building during the 1946 Calcutta riots, when 4,000 people lost their lives and 100,000 people lost their homes, all over the course of seventy-two hours. My Dida must have seen the bloodshed, Tapati Mashi was probably by her side, only eleven years old at the time. Did she look over the edge of my Dida's roof and cower with fear at the knowledge that humans could inflict such extreme violence upon each other? Upon the bodies of women? How did that realization—that fear—affect my Tapati Mashi's psyche? How can I map the ways in which that violence and colonialism affected them all?

Most of all: how does a mother care for a child in the face of such violence?

'You know, Rani, we saw such things,' my Dida would say as she stared out of her bedroom window. Her eyes were fixed on something I could not see—perhaps the ghosts of people torn and quartered; the remains of body parts languishing in the city; saris and undergarments littered across streets; women's bodies branded with nationalist slogans—this, a full-blown exhibition of how women were being treated like the new cartography of India, fragmented, cut and abandoned.

The culmination of years of colonial rule—manifesting itself as a crazed assault. Years of Indians being told that they were inadequate had ignited inconceivable violence between people who look like one another.

I cannot imagine the impact that witnessing such violence had on my Dida and her children. What I do understand is this—that my Tapati Mashi, worn down by colonialism, eroded by nationalism and demolished by patriarchy, was a siren that followed my mother to the United States. And when my mother became a widow, the reservoir in her mind broke. There was no way to protect herself from the history that clung to her neurons like plaque. Motherhood must have furthered her decay.

Until, one day, she was left rotting.

My Dida was married at twelve in an arranged set-up to a man ten years her senior—my Dadu, my mother's father. She birthed eight children with him, her first at only fifteen or so, when she was still a child herself. Gender determined the lives of her children. As my mother believed, boys were better—no dowry, no fear of pregnancy before marriage and no worries about becoming a curse on the family name. I know now, even if she never admitted it, that my mother believed madness was gendered, too, and hysteria lived only in the psyches of women.

My Dadu left my Dida to become a monk after most of their children were grown. He died in his sleep before I was born, the most peaceful death that anyone in the family would experience.

The older I got, the more I realized how much beauty determined the way my Dida loved her children. She herself was not conventionally beautiful. Melasma splattered her skin, dark patches of melanin. Hunchbacked, her body traced a fine arc, her head permanently thrust down. Most of the time, she didn't wear a bra. Eight suckling children had stretched her breasts, which hung low, slapping against her body. She didn't seem to care about her 'unattractiveness'. She had grown into it, so much so that she seemed to purposely grow more uncomely each year. The arc in her back became more defined. The spots that splattered her face grew darker. She blamed her children as if they were parasites that had buried parts of themselves in her womb, so that even after their birth, they engendered her physical appearance.

My Dida might not have cared about her own outward form, but she certainly cared about how her daughters looked. Their beauty seemed to give her own plainness absolution. They were a lifeline to the attractiveness that she believed she had not been given. She was particularly obsessed with their complexion, in a nation where fairness equates to allure. The stories my mother told me of her family's hardships were plenty, but one has always haunted me. My Jayashree Mashi was my Dida's least parsha—fair-skinned—daughter and she was treated differently as a result. 'I was given the head, Jayashree Mashi the tail,' my mother said, as she explained how the fish was distributed. At the time, I didn't fully understand what her story meant. Now I do—that, for Bengalis, the head is the best and most savoury part, and to serve the head to someone is to acknowledge how important that person is in the household. The fact that Jayashree Mashi was given the tail—the part with the least meat, devoid of the delectable morsels of buttery fish—spoke of my Dida's hatred for her dark skin.

It is, of course, difficult to pin down the root cause of colourism in India. Some blame it on the caste system—though there are different tones of skin in every community regardless of caste, and my own aunts were a panoply of shades. What can't be dismissed is the role of British colonialism in the cultivation of colourism in South Asia—the fact that the British proselytized light skin as a sociocultural ideology. How can anyone ignore how the modern world was, and is, shaped by imperial design? And, no matter the precise root of colourism in India, in my family, the origin was clear—the British were the root of my Dida's adoration of fair skin.

So naturally, being half-white made me the favourite of her grandchildren—she adored me and I adored her in return. During my visits, I would lie next to her on a narrow single bed framed with metal that reminded me of a hospital gurney. I would look out of the window beside her bed and gaze into our neighbour's house. I would watch as they lived their lives, cooked their food, fought and embraced. Dida told me stories about rajas and ranis, she'd discuss the Mahabharata and the Bhagavad Gita, Ram and Sita, Hanuman and Ganesh, the olden days of British rule and perfection. To me, her mind was expansive, filled with tales and adventures. She was a resource, a storybook. I asked her questions and imagined the characters that she narrated. *Dida, why is Ganesh part elephant? How can Hanuman fly?*

She travelled to California to be with my mother and me when my father was diagnosed with cancer. She was happy with the prospect of a cleaner, brighter, whiter place to inhabit, and cared for me and my father. She held my father in her arms as he took his last breath.

But she didn't like the United States. Pasadena was not London. It was not Britain. Pasadena was too modern and spread out. There were no metro stations that allowed her to travel and she did not know how to drive.

'*Amar London beshi pochhondo!*' she would say. 'I love London more!'

But none of her children lived in London. Her dream of being a British citizen would never come true.

Violence was my Dida and mother's love language. Fights between them were as melodramatic as a Bollywood movie. They often began over nothing. Or something inconsequential. As a child, I could not tell the difference. Now, I know those fights were the result of some past betrayal or upset. Jealousy frequently seemed to be at the heart of the animosity. Jealousy and money. In a single moment, my mother could become the target of so much anger. In those moments, my mother radically transformed from my Dida's favourite beautiful daughter to her most bitter enemy.

In Kolkata, after seeing Tapati Mashi in the asylum, my mother had grown increasingly distraught. For days, she did not leave my Dida's flat. Instead, she lay on our bed and stared at the ceiling fan, tracking its blades as they spun round and round; it was as though their movement offered security. How utterly ironic that, years later, she would lie on the same bed, staring at the same fan, in a state of squalor.

When my mother woke up from her stupor, she was angry. My Dida was angry too. At seven, I didn't know why. Now I know that my Dida was angry because she could see the phantom of my Tapati Mashi hovering over my mother.

'*Tomar ki matha kharap?*' my Dida yelled. 'Are you crazy?'

'Na!' my mother yelled back.

I sat upright on the bed my mother had slept in as a child. My back was flat against the wall. I was half-frightened, half-comfortable, a spectator to this event, a fight that mimicked so many others I had seen before it. No matter how familiar the choreography, they always frightened me. The women continued to yell, my mother's face a shade of red that only comes from rage. She enumerated everything my Dida had ever done to hurt her. My Dida dripped with sweat and responded with every sacrifice she had ever made for my mother.

Suddenly, my Dida stuck out her tongue to convey the shame and disgust she felt for my mother. Long gasps of breath left her body as she kept that tongue out for what seemed like forever. My Dida had tipped over into lunacy. She pulled my mother's arm, jerking it down as though trying to rip it from its socket. My mother yelled. I jumped off the bed and ran towards them. I needed to protect my mother from my Dida's words and fists.

'Dida, please stop!' I begged.

My mother held my grandmother's arm and inched towards her hot tongue, which was still out, wagging about. My Dida heaved in disgust. They were almost nose-to-nose. I stepped between them. My mother pushed me aside and my knees knocked into the wooden frame of the bed beside us. I yelled, echoing my mother's scream, but to them I was irrelevant. I trailed back to my place as silent spectator. I held my knees and hoped the violence wouldn't escalate. In those moments, with these two impossibly strong women battling to settle old scores, for what they had done to each other, and for what had been done to them, nothing felt safe.

As an adult, I look back at these moments and question how much of the rage was a product of history, and how much was biological. I think about how the biological and historical interact, like two bits entangled, each affected by the other regardless of the distance in time or space. I think of the choices and events that affected members of my family—members whom I never met—passed down to my Dida, my mother and me. I think of the ribbons of our DNA tying us to our past. Now, I wish I had a medical reasoning for my Dida's behaviour and my mother's, a name for their afflictions, but they never sought help, denying us any diagnostic answer.

I only know that through this bind, my Dida taught my mother that love was defined by conflict; care was bestowed through prohibition, fear and rage. At first, I felt repulsed by my Dida and mother, both of whom turned unsightly when enraged. Now, a part of me feels pangs of empathy for my Dida. I see how my Dida's story of being a child bride, the tumultuous forces of colonialism and war, and biology all played a part in her inability to unconditionally love her children and how much that caused my mother to become the mother she was.

A few nights after we returned home to the United States, I awoke to find my mother sitting on the edge of the bed, her hand inching towards mine. I looked through the crack between the curtains, trying to discern the colour of the sky. The night was steadfast in its darkness—only a slice of moonlight cut through the room. Small patches of sweat seeped through my mother's pink nightgown. Her back looked like a map, the sweaty imprints forming nations and continents, a cartography of fear.

'Can you hear them?' my mother asked. 'There are soldiers marching on the roof.'

I gazed up at the white stucco ceiling. I strained to listen, to hear the noise my mother heard, but I couldn't hear anything at all.

'Yes, Mama, I hear them'—whoever 'they' were.

I wanted to hear them. I wanted to protect my mother from whatever monsters were plaguing her. My mother finally stopped trembling. She laughed and lifted the covers to crawl back in bed with me. As she slept soundly, I stared at the ceiling, listening still for soldiers who were not marching across our roof.

Five years before I flew across the world to save my mother, I went looking through my mother's house, frantically searching for documents like a power of attorney that would allow me to be her caretaker. I needed something that would give me authority over her medical care and enable me to protect her from anyone who could take advantage of her. But I did not find any such documents. Instead, I found an abandoned letter in which she attempted to chronicle her life:

I grew up in Calcutta. I lived in England, Germany and Switzerland and then America. I was very beautiful. But I grew old and could not get rid of my belly which was not nice.

Sometimes, I heard soldiers marching on the roof of my home. I was so frightened of them. But then, I realized, it was god telling me I needed to lose weight!!!!!

He was trying to heal me.

WINTER 2015
CONFESSION

WHEN I RECEIVED THE MESSAGE that I needed to fly to India to rescue my mother, I did not go right away. Perhaps this is what I led you to believe, embarrassed that I did not drop everything and run to save my mother. The truth is, I received the message from my cousin on 23 November. But I did not leave until the end of December. There are many reasons—I was enrolled in a networking programme designed to help people leave their profession to find a job in the world of start-ups. The last few weeks of the year were filled with introductions to companies and the promise of a new career, everything I had been working for.

You see, my dream of becoming an academic had evaporated; I had been searching for a tenure-track position for eight years but could not find a job. Universities were staffing most of their courses with adjuncts, slowly replacing the tenured dinosaurs as they retired or died. I fled to the supposed greener pastures of the tech world. Instead of thinking about post-colonial theory, I spent my days learning about company culture and the language of marketing. I made ends meet by waitressing, with my tips supplemented by unemployment benefits.

But deep down, and you may have already guessed this, what lay at the core of my hesitation to leave for India was the fear of the heat, the smoke of that house on fire. I did not want to see my mother again.

So, when I got Niraj's message, I called Rima Mashi one last time, to see if she could care for my mother for the next few weeks. Would my mother be okay if I waited? Was she on death's door? Could I finish my programme and mentally prepare myself to see my mother once again?

Was I using my search for a new career as an excuse to not go?

I sat on my bed, gripping my phone. 'I can come in December, is that okay?' I asked, hoping Rima Mashi would reassure me that my mother was fine. I was not unlike an infant who desperately seeks a milk bottle or stuffed rabbit to hold.

'I will take care of her,' Rima Mashi said.

'Okay,' I replied. 'I'll be there in a month.'

A month later, sitting in the ambulance with my mother's frail body, I cannot tell if my tears are from guilt or grief. My mother looks up at me with what I can only describe as love. It is a shock to finally feel my mother's love. An utterly foreign sensation. I wipe off the pearls of sweat from her forehead and tears drip from my eyes. The remaining threads of her hair, gold and silver, twinkle as we race past streetlights and all the beeping cars.

I look down at my mother with devotion and fear. This is my fault, I think. The horror of my neglect overwhelms me. I did not do the work of a Good Indian Daughter and care for my mother. I did not fulfil my role as her court-appointed guardian. I chose to ignore her condition, protecting myself from her, foisting the responsibility onto my aunt. I am the reason my mother is dying.

The flames lick at both our feet.

4

IN GRADE SCHOOL, MY CLASSMATES would talk about all the toys they had asked for from Santa at Christmas time—Tonka trucks and blonde Barbies in bright pink dresses. They'd tell me how they'd lay out chocolate chip cookies and pints of milk in front of their real fir trees, the spicy smell of balsam and cinnamon filling the air. They'd wake to find boxes wrapped in metallic silver, green and red paper, tied with curly bows beneath the tree. The boxes affirmed that they were good children, deserving of Mr Claus's attention. I wanted to feel like that too—a good girl who got presents from a big-bellied man with a white beard.

My mother mostly ignored American holidays. She preferred Bengali celebrations like Durga Pujo. Pujo was a time when Kolkata would burst into a kaleidoscope of colours, with thousands of devotees carrying massive effigies of Durga to the Ganga and immersing them into the river. But there were also times when my mother *did* want to fit in with the other moms at school and follow American customs.

One year, I asked why Santa Claus never came to our house and if she could have him visit. I searched the house, hoping my mother had hidden some presents. I found a few in our utility closet. On top of each was my mother's distinctive cursive handwriting: 'To: Rani, From: Santa.' I was thrilled that my mother had done what I had asked for and, at the same time, sad that I already knew Santa Claus wasn't real. When she saw me with the closet door open, peering at the gifts with hope and melancholy, she said, 'I tried.' Even back then, I understood how hard it was for her to accommodate traditions that weren't hers.

It was 1984, and Cabbage Patch Kids ruled the toy market. The news splashed stories of mothers fighting over the dolls, riots breaking out in stores, parents driving hundreds of miles to find one for their kids. The lore around the dolls fuelled their popularity. They had been born in a cabbage patch, and when you bought one, it came with its own little outfit, a certificate of adoption, and a birth certificate—as if to assure each young child that their new baby had blossomed from the fertile soil of America.

I had pined for more than a year because all the other girls at school had one. The dolls were a badge of belonging and I so frantically wanted to belong. Now, as the presents from our utility closet lay under our frosted fake Christmas tree, wreathed in a rainbow of lights, I hoped desperately that my very own Cabbage Patch Doll would be in one of those brightly wrapped boxes. When I opened one, I stared into round blue eyes set inside a pudgy pale face. I touched the doll's sunshine yellow hair, made from strands of rough yarn, and admired its signature overbite. I imagined my mother yanking the doll from another mother's arms in her quest to satisfy my deepest desires. Or perhaps she had woken at six in the morning and driven to Toys "R" Us, waiting for the store to open. That day, my mother was a superhero who had captured the holy grail. It was a magical Christmas. I embraced these moments like a squirrel hoarding acorns. They were memories that kept me warm when winter arrived.

A few months later, we were out shopping at Fedco, our local wholesale department store.

'Mama, can I get a new My Little Pony?' I traced my fingers across horses in lavenders, soft pinks and pastel yellows. Their long, synthetic tails tickled the edges of my hand. My request for this toy was involuntary. When my eyes reached the toy aisle, my desires revealed themselves with words I didn't even realize I had actually spoken.

'You are spoiled! I gave you a Cabbage Patch Doll. I didn't even have a doll when I was young! You have too many toys,' my mother yelled, her voice so high that I imagined the aisles of glassware shattering all around us.

Exposed like that, in a department store littered with people pushing their shopping carts around us as they perused the products perfectly lined on the shelves, I felt as though even the inanimate objects were staring at us. The miniature pastel horses, their oval eyes wider than before, gawked at me. I wanted to be invisible.

'I'm sorry, Mama,' I said, my eyes brimming with tears. I had not yet learned the mechanisms used to prevent crying—clenching the jaw; dropping the head to help close the throat; concentrating on any muscle that could divert energy, so water didn't pour from the eyes.

'Why are you *crying*?' she yelled.

I flinched. I succumbed to the knowledge that she was my mother, even while dreading what was to come. She grabbed my wrist and twisted it. A piercing pain shot to my joint at the forceful bending of my flesh. I stopped crying.

My mother dragged me through the store. At the checkout line, she threw milk, fruits and vegetables onto the conveyor belt, her grip still tight around my wrist. She finally let go when we reached our car, a beat-up, royal blue Honda. I curled into my seat silently. I realized that no one would rescue me. That she was the only caretaker I had.

She was angry throughout the entire car ride home.

When we reached our driveway, she slammed on the brakes, and my body lunged forward, braced by the seatbelt. I got out of the car silently, wincing as the rust that had formed along the door hinges let out a long squeal. I feared even my footsteps might stoke her anger.

No sooner had I reached the cold Spanish tiles of the entryway than she threw the brown grocery bags against the floor, blueberries falling out of their container. They patterned the tiles with inky dots. A carton of milk went sliding down the hall.

'Where are you going?' she yelled.

'My room,' I whispered.

'You won't be going *anywhere*!'

She reached for my ear lobe and pulled. I could hear my ear pop so loudly I started to feel dizzy. When I wobbled, she let go, grabbed my arm instead and yanked it again. I remembered my Dida reaching for my mother's hand the same way, the times I had watched the strongest women I had known fight each other, history spewing from their mouths and saliva patterning their lips like braille.

My mother finally let go. I ran to my room, slammed the door and turned the lock, twisting it frantically to make sure it stayed securely fastened, the same way we had secured the doors each day against the Night Stalker. I hurried into my closet and shut the wooden door. Inside, I put my back against the wall and slid down, my knees folded. I held them tightly, my wrist and arm throbbing, my ear still ringing. I could hear her footsteps, each press of her three-inch heels against the tile floor. She reached my door and began to bang. My tears could not be controlled. My body hurt. My eyelids shut to obscure my gaze. My mother could hear my deep breaths, my sobs. She could hear everything, always.

'Open this door! Why are you crying?' She seemed baffled by my reaction. My tears were beyond her comprehension.

I put my hands to my ears to muffle the sound of her fists thumping against the plywood.

The lightlessness I felt inside the closet was reassuring. My body had faded into that dark space that smelled like nothing. All that reminded me I was alive were the stabs of pain. How much time passed as my hands remained pressed to my ears, my eyes shut, the tears falling? I do not know.

When I finally let go of my ears and opened my eyes, guiding the door of my closet open, my mother was no longer there. I tried to quietly move through space.

She was in her bedroom. I crept down the hallway and peeked in. She sat at the edge of her bed, her hands braced on her mattress, her vision directed outside the glass doors. The sun was slowly moving down to the edges of the Earth, a blur of orange and pink. She shook her head over and over.

'No. Leave me, please,' she cried. She raised her hands to her hair and pulled as if she were trying to extricate something from her mind.

'Mama?' I said.

I didn't know if she could hear me, but she slowly stopped shaking her head and opened her eyes. She mumbled to herself again, 'No, no, no, no, no.' She raised her right hand to her hair and began to pull as if she might remove the strands and follicle, the skin, and expose the layers of her brain, all mush and blood. I no longer cared if I made a sound. I dashed over to sit beside her. I grabbed the same hand that had pulled my arm and ear and moved it away from her head. I held it gently.

'It's okay, Mama,' I said as I tried to calm her from whatever spirits were inside.

She lifted her legs onto the mattress. Her head fell to her pillow.

'Sleep with me?' she asked.

I positioned myself within the alcove of her body, my ear and arm still pulsating. She put her arm around me, and I closed my eyes. Asleep, I dreamt of the pastel-coloured ponies. They grew into giant beasts with ginormous legs that threatened to squish me, their eyes as big as blimps. I wondered how I had provoked my mother's fury, and plotted all the ways I could relieve her suffering mind.

It was always rage that sparked my mother's hallucinations, which would later completely take over her mind. It was as though the neurons in her brain were crying out, frantically echoing the horrors of the past—the horrors of her family and the horrors of history.

Much later, I would go on to study colonial history to contextualize my mother's behaviour. I would learn about a nation's past, so I could rationalize my mother's actions, her mental health and the way she brought me up.

The effects of my Dida's preference for light skin were mapped onto my mother's body, which became a reproductive vehicle that gave me life. My mother's light skin ensured that the family's lineage would be lighter, better—according to the colonizer—closer to whiteness but never *entirely* white. Which meant that my mother and everyone in her bloodline would forever be chasing an elusive promise of beauty, a kind of civility embodied by the ones who ruled India for over two centuries.

Was my mouth, which craved my mother's breast as an infant, the last straw? Too much had been demanded of her already. And when my father died, she was all alone.

Today, I understand the context of my mother's fury. But as a young girl, I couldn't help but wonder: was my mother angry because I was a bad child?

And most rotten of all: maybe she didn't love me because I didn't deserve to be loved.

It didn't strike me: perhaps she didn't have the capacity to love at all.

5

I WAS EIGHT YEARS OLD the day my mother became an American citizen. I waited for her at the kitchen window, wide-eyed and alert, my palms sticky from a bowl of mango and milk sprinkled with brown sugar—a treat that was a constant in our home. My face was whiskered with mango meat, my smile broad.

'Mama is going to be like me!' I yelled out to my babysitter, Lydia, who smiled and said, 'Yes, yes she is.'

I was overwhelmed by the prospect that my mother, the woman I wanted more than anything to look like and be, was going to share the connection of national belonging with me, even if I didn't fully understand what that meant. I had noticed that we were treated differently at airports. When it came to immigration lines, my navy-blue booklet was stamped quickly, without worry, as if the eagle etched upon it was a god who granted me entrance into different worlds. When it was my mother's turn, the four Asiatic lions didn't grant passage in the same way. I thought of those lions as guardians to the magical land of Narnia, where majestic animals talked and colourful morsels of Turkish delight abounded. For the men who sat behind enclosed wooden desks, who decided which people could come into their country and which could not, my mother's passport was not an enchanted booklet. Her turn always took longer than mine. The immigration officers eyed her up and down, assessing her beauty and ethnicity. I saw them silently question whether she was a woman who could wreak havoc in their land. I recognized, on some subconscious level, that having an American passport made travel easier for me.

It was later, when I thought more deeply about the issue, that I realized that no actual lines were drawn on Earth; no physical demarcations showed that borders were real and tangible. All that illustrated national boundaries were the soldiers and police officers who stood at airports, watching.[1]

When I saw our car pull into our driveway, there was a stranger behind the wheel. As she got out, I was perplexed. Who was this woman? She was short like my mother, but her gait was somehow different and so were her clothes. My mother was fashionable. She wore chic '70s outfits—shirts in bright yellow, purple and turquoise, jeans that accentuated her thin body and small waistline. She made her own floor-length dresses in bold prints. She swirled her long hair, which grew to her waist, into a tight knot that sat neatly upon her head. This woman was not fashionable. Her grey skirt was pleated and unflattering. Her shirt, a muddy colour, was misshapen and too big for her petite shoulders. Mostly, it was the woman's hair that stayed with me. Hers was short and frizzy unlike my mother's drape of shiny satin locks that, when left open, hung all the way to her waist.

'Lydia, where is Mama?'

'No, no, Rangeela, that *is* your mama. She just cut her hair.' While the familiarness of her words and the inflection in her voice were soothing, I was still horrified. My mother's face appeared rounder and plumper, her cheekbones no longer accentuated by her elegant tresses. She had cut off that which made her special—the dark blanket I nestled my face in at night. The loss of my mother's hair overwhelmed me. My chest beat a loud rhythm that only I could hear. My eyes watered from shock and loss. I shrieked and felt my tonsils vibrate.

My mother rushed into the house. She did not think her daughter would have such a visceral reaction to her altered appearance. She was my mother, and that was all that mattered. But I had learned from both her and my Dida that the way she looked meant everything. I looked up into this stranger's face and asked, 'Where is Mama?'

'It's me, sona, it's me.' She had my mother's voice.

She explained that she needed to find a job. The money my father had left us was running out.

I was too young to understand money—how it was spent, the ways that it was needed to sustain lives. I was too young to understand that my mother's beauty and marriage to my white father had conferred on my childhood an immense amount of financial privilege.

'But why … does … that mean … you had to cut your hair?'

'I have to look more like an American now. I *am* an American now,' my mother said, resigned.

Like many immigrants, particularly at that time, gaining citizenship was an unequal transaction, much like the exchange rate of rupees to dollars. In the United States, you needed to give up your culture to assimilate into white America, even though as an immigrant of colour, my mother would never be able to do so. I know my mother believed it was an obligation that she Americanize herself, try to shed her accent, dress like wealthy white women, cut her hair into a 'modern' bob. Most importantly, she believed that 'fitting in' was the only way to acquire financial independence, which, of course, was true in the United States, where to be like the white majority was more or less the only way to succeed—so much for the myth of the American Dream. How ironic that my mother had left a country where colonialism had demanded its members approximate whiteness, only to enter another one that did as well—another nation where the idea of democracy is rooted in the lie of a melting pot where everyone is welcomed, but no one really is at all. The double demands of American assimilation and British colonialism were too much for my mother's mind.

At the time, I didn't fully comprehend what it meant for my mother to *be* an American, to relinquish a heritage (at least outwardly) that was bound to her very being—her name, her hair, her accent. To this day, I cannot know the full psychic cost she paid for her attempts at assimilation. What I do know is that she never considered herself successful in her efforts; she told me as much when I reached adulthood. While my mother could curate her clothes, how she spoke and her name, she could not change her ethnicity, she could not alter her mind, her history, her way of moving through the world. I felt her simultaneous desire to blend yet absolute inability to do so. How torturous it must have been.

When my mother became a US citizen, she changed her name from Shukla to Sue and became a real estate agent for Century 21. She shuffled around her office in the hope of selling homes and reaping real estate commissions. Her new career took up most of her time and I became her little helper. I accompanied her door-to-door to hand out flyers for house listings. She dispensed her cards to whomever would take them. We never went to the fanciest of neighbourhoods, where million-dollar homes lined the leafy, well-tended roads, with manicured backyards and pools designed to look like real lagoons. Rather, my mother canvassed neighbourhoods where the pools glowed the garish blue you see flying over cities that remain warm year-round. She somehow knew that wealthy agents who drove BMWs and carried designer purses commanded the affluent part of the real estate world. Even though her English was fluent, she couldn't completely hide her Bengali accent, and she sensed it wasn't welcome in neighbourhoods with pools so stylish they resembled lakes.

I often wondered what people's lives looked like inside the walls of the houses my mother sold. I imagined nuclear families with two children—one boy and one girl—whose parents kissed their silky ginger and blonde heads every morning before school as they ate blueberry pancakes dripping with dewy maple syrup served on heavy ceramic plates. For dinner: mashed potatoes covered in thick gravy, pork chops drizzled with mealy apple sauce and mossy green frozen peas. My mother was not preoccupied with such thoughts. She just needed the homes to sell so she could support us.

'We must pray to god that I get a good commission for this house.' That was her mantra.

People eyed my mother and her symmetrical face. Some women cracked open their doors. Their fear dissipated when they saw me, a young child. But still, they always rejected my mother's card—*not interested!* Some men swung their doors wide open, rivetted by my mother's presence. They took her card. 'Sue? What's your *real* name?' Some men would call and list their homes to ask her out, but she was careful in her assessment of new clients. She knew that some of these men had wives and others were not wealthy enough—and she wanted financial stability.

Her style changed. On workdays, she entirely gave up the second-hand '70s skirts and dresses with loud patterns, the platform shoes that lengthened her legs and gave her the illusion of height beyond her mere five feet. She exchanged all this lavish colour for a conservative '80s aesthetic, as she had that day she became an American citizen—button-up shirts in dull brown or navy-blue with boxy shoulder pads; drab corduroy skirts the colour of vomit; round-toed pumps that rubbed against her heels and scraped off her flesh. She would run home and slather her wounds in coconut oil, bandage herself up and ask if I would lie with her as she rested her legs. She only wore saris and salwar kameezes during our time in India or on the weekends, when we took our trips to LA's Little India, where she fell back into being Shukla Buku—Shukla her proper name, Buku her dak-nam, the pet name only those close to you call you.

The real estate market was flourishing in California. Soon she made additions to our home—new curtains that hung heavy against the floor, the kind of lush carpets you could sink your toes into, a deck and Jacuzzi installed in our backyard that was meant to soothe our bodies while we watched the sun set across the Los Angeles skyline. The smog in Southern California created the most spectacular nightfall; streaks of sapphire, lavender and plum wiped across the horizon like elegant strokes of a paint brush. Sometimes, the sky was brilliant coral, sunshine yellow and flaming orange, a canvas of light.

'We need to add value to our house!' my mother said each time she made a renovation. There was a confidence in her voice from her newly acquired profession, and while she scuttled about and searched for new clients, she had less time to be angry with me.

Sometimes I wonder why my mother never moved us back to India, where we wouldn't have been all alone. I know the autonomy of having a job was part of her reason for staying in California, as was the threat of being a widow in India, which would come with its own brutal set of punishments and easily lead to Tapati Mashi's fate. Being in India would also have meant fighting my Dida, living on the rim of a volcano day after day.

I can see all my mother was running from, but I still wonder: what was she running towards?

By the time I was ten years old, my desire to be by mother's side night and day began to dwindle. I wanted to be with other girls my age. I wanted to smell them and hang out with them. Not my mother. I wanted slumber parties and American movies. Not Bollywood films and trips to India. I wanted to watch television and talk on the phone with the girls at school who were pretty and popular. To be like them. To be near them.

Blonde hair and blue eyes were the physical attributes I most coveted. I wanted these girls' light, milky skin and strawberry hair, their rosy complexions, and their ability to blush. My olive skin, which turned a deep brown in the Southern Californian sun, never betrayed any flush of embarrassment. The sun highlighted my coffee-coloured hair with sienna stripes. It was not gold and glistening like the valley girls'. Rather, I had to wear my hair like an Indian school kid—two pigtails with ribbons entwined in each braid.

Each morning, my mother would sit me down and plait my hair to create a proper and controlled Indian child. She'd apply coconut oil into my scalp to make my locks grow and shine. She bought different coloured ribbons—purple, pink, green and red—and she'd weave them into each braid. My face was long with sharp edges, a pointy nose and large eyes—hazel with specks of green and amber, but only if you looked into them and asked, 'What colour are her eyes?'

When the favoured girls finally agreed to a play date at my house, they smelled the mustard seeds that popped in hot oil, and the sharp, floral notes of garam masala that my mother sometimes used to cook her torkaris in. They saw the Hindu gods and godmen that hung on walls around our house—Kali and Sai Baba. The day after their visit, they spread word around school that my mother and I were strange.

'Rani's house smells funny. There are scary monsters on her walls. She's gross and dirty.'

After that, I was excluded from parties and sleepovers. But I persisted in my desire to be around those girls. I continued to call them, despite their mean words and callous actions. I was stubborn, almost unafraid of their talent for cruelty.

My tenacity paid off, because as time passed and they forgot about my strange home filled with foreign objects, they began inviting me over again. I existed in a between-space of acceptance and rejection. I spun in a merry-go-round of being wanted and unwanted.

Though I longed to fit in, a part of me also wanted to be different. I knew I would never be white or blonde, the epitome of 1980s beauty. To be noticed, I needed to stand out both in personality and style. My need for originality was a manifestation of my desire for these girls to *see* me.

I didn't realize that my desire to be unique also stemmed from my mother's identity. Though she made every effort to assimilate, she still clung to her roots. Beyond that complicated duality of wanting to change and wanting to remain the same, my mother was fundamentally different from most people. She never fit in anywhere; she was too much of a spectacle, too unruly, too charming, too loud. She was too much herself to blend in. She stood out from everyone, everywhere she went—in how she laughed a belly-deep laugh that made her snort; in how she could walk up to people and engage with them even if they showed disdain; in how she failed to hide her jealousy or her desires; and especially in how her anger remained uncontrollable and plain for all to see. Over the years, her temper became swifter and fiercer, her voice louder, her accent stronger and her laugh deeper. To her core, my mother was both formidable and alluring. Around my girlfriends, I found myself adopting her persona. My mother was unforgettable. And even at that age I knew—there is no worse fate than being forgotten.

The girls at school must have known that I could not be completely discarded. For a month, I'd spend my days alone, ostracized and isolated, but then, a month later, I'd spend time with the popular girls again, dancing to Madonna and Cyndi Lauper at their slumber parties. The following month, their affections and interest in me would wane, and I'd be on my own again. The pattern became as cyclical as the seasons—which didn't really exist in Southern California.

My favourite pillow came from India. It was three feet long, cylindrical and covered in red felt, plush but hard as well, with a firmness similar to that of a human. I still shared a bed with my mother, but as I grew into puberty, I began to gravitate towards this pillow. At night, I'd rub myself against the plush covering and stimulate something I didn't have a name for. An exquisite sensation pulsed through my body, a feeling that I was nearing something unique, covetable and hard to reach. I also implicitly understood that what I was doing was wrong. I didn't know how I knew this—I just did. Something so very desirous couldn't possibly be permissible.

One early morning, when I was nine, my mother woke to find me next to her, my body moving against my red pillow, my face squished against its soft felt, my arms holding it close. She raised herself off the bed to turn on the bedside lamp. A silence fell over her. I noticed that her hair was dishevelled and strands of gooey sleep stuck to the edges of her mouth. With the soft brush of her palm, she delicately wiped the goo away. The glow of the rising sun peeked in from the crack between her bedroom drapes and formed a hazy spotlight around her.

I felt the revealing morning light on my own body and I stiffened. My breath grew short and my body bristled as I awaited punishment. But my mother did not speak. Instead, in a quiet, soft burst of movement, she simply lay back on the bed and lifted her floral nightgown, pink and blue with a background of grey. She showed me her body.

Her flesh was layered and moist. Brown and dark, almost blue with a tinge of purple, like a bruise. What I saw was cavernous and frightening. A tunnel into her insides, leading to her organs and the place where I once resided. She spoke as she displayed herself, her head on her pillow, her face tilted down so she could see my reaction—ensuring I was paying attention. She told me this was a special region, and I shouldn't share it with anyone. This was my flower. It had to remain untouched and unscathed, protected and private.

'Men will try and take this flower from you. Don't let them, not until marriage,' she said.

Seeing my mother exposed was at once captivating and terrifying. Her vagina was dark with sticky flaps of skin, and induced in me, so young, a palpable sense of horror. I shuddered on witnessing the bare fleshiness, the way the entirety of her being felt reduced to one measured body part. Rather than being my mother—a woman with high cheekbones and almond eyes; a woman with a temper to abolish all tempers; a woman who possessed charm and made men's heads turn when she walked past—she instantaneously collapsed into a biological fragment. It was as if a serial killer had invaded our home and mutilated her body into individual limbs. I desperately wanted to put her back together again. I wanted to look away.

I understood that my mother thought the gesture was a warning, a stop sign, a signal to be chaste. At that age, her lesson worked—I was terrified. But fear builds a boundary, and boundaries beg to be toyed with, crossed and broken. Her description of the region, and the sensations it received, as unique and discreet, *also* illustrated that this part of her—of me—was extraordinary, and I needed to start exploring it.

As my nascent sexuality grew, so did the distance between my mother and me.

Later, when I became a teenager, and then an adult, my mother and I would fight about sex, my future, my behaviour, my life.

'You don't know what it was like being a single mother all alone. I had to please myself! I had no one! I could only use my hand!' she would yell.

I see that my mother believed that if you had to explore your sexuality, and were unmarried, you were better off exploring it on your own, providing yourself with self-regulating pleasure not conditioned by coupling, not determined by partnership. It was lonelier, but safer. You wouldn't risk the shame, the gossip that came from being a woman who was 'loose'. My mother was determined that I would be a proper girl with a proper life, even if she herself hadn't been one, or had one.

I don't know if my mother remembered that dawn. But I will forever think of the moment as her attempt to hold on to me. She knew that my pulsating body was a fraying rope, and I would no longer be her anchor. I'd let her get lost at sea.

6

THE SALESPEOPLE WHO ONCE SAT in cubicles in my mother's Century 21 office were no longer there. The ring of phones, the babble of voices, the excitement of prosperity, vanished. Thin stacks of papers were scattered in dishevelled piles, as if a tiny windstorm had passed through the space. My mother and a few other agents drifted around a room that once had held fifteen employees.

The real estate market in California had slowed down and my mother was becoming increasingly anxious. I sat in a chair and pouted, bored, rolling my eyes at the barren office space. I was not interested in the real estate crisis and my mother's worries about how to keep us afloat. I was eleven and I no longer called her Mama.

'Ma, can I get some frozen yogurt?'

My mother grabbed her purse without looking at me and searched for some change.

I snatched the pile of coins with glee and skipped out the front door into the warm Southern Californian evening. A hint of the Santa Ana winds skimmed my face. My mother's office was smack-dab in the middle of a long block lined with office buildings, strip malls and a McDonald's that always smelled like French fries. I walked outside, looking left and then right. Each crosswalk seemed miles away from me, and the yogurt shop was four lanes ahead.

I saw the cars zoom by and waited. The first two lanes were clear. I ran to the yellow line and stopped, peering to my right as a pickup truck slowed down to a halt. The man driving gestured for me to go. I smiled at him and darted past his bumper. That's when something huge flew into me. My body moved up steel, then glass, and tumbled back down. I fell in spirals through a tunnel of nothingness and plummeted into night.

When I woke up, I was holding my right arm up, but I didn't know why. The coins I had so securely carried were scattered around the dark concrete, flickering from the reflection of the lights above. People ran towards me as I stood up to move towards the sidewalk.

'Are you okay? Oh my god, someone call 911. That car ran right into her!'

I reached the side of the road and sat down to absorb the voices and the sound of cars that slowed down to see what had happened. That's when I felt the pain in my right arm, a sharp, unbearable pain that made me sweat. My eyes clenched and my dark blue nails dug into my skin.

'Shit,' I said out loud, though softly. It was the first time I'd ever cursed.

My mother was understandably hysterical as she ran across the street to check that I was alive. During the ambulance drive to the hospital, she held my hand and stared at my nails, which I had painted a shimmering navy-blue that morning. She shook her head. She had told me, she reminded me, that dark colours invited misfortune.

You shouldn't have worn this colour nail polish. I told you it was bad luck.

The force of three thousand pounds had broken my humerus bone.

In the aftermath of the accident, my mother was furious at me for jaywalking. At first, it was my dark nail polish that had caused it. Then, it was just me being a disobedient girl. It was true that I had become a bratty prepubescent—desperately wanting attention from girls and boys at school; shying away from my mother when she wished to spend time with me—and my mother chose to point it out.

The cast made me popular. 'Oh my god, what happened? Tell us everything,' all the popular kids said, as if being near me made them special, because I had survived the rare experience of tumbling up and down the front end of a vehicle. My new cast was a brilliant white canvas for my classmates to write their way into my spectacular story. Everyone wanted to sign it. But soon, the allure of a new cast wore off. Black and red ink swirled across it until it looked dirty. The lustre of my story began to fade.

At first, my popularity was thrilling. I was excited to be the centre of attention at school, not just the centre of my mother's anger at home. But when my popularity began to wane, I was stuck waiting for a friend to call or anticipating my mother's anger. I longed for the brrrring of our phone. I wanted to pick up the receiver and hear a classmate's voice, inviting me to a sleepover. Without the fantasy of having friends, I had to confront the extreme loneliness of my childhood.

'You think your friends will take care of you? Who will support you? Me. No one else but me,' my mother would say, over and over again. I knew she was right. The only person I had in the world was her.

A few months later, I stood in a courtroom, my arm in a cast and sling, my mother next to me, as a judge assessed the settlement offer from the woman whose car had hit me. My fingernails were no longer dark blue.

Although I had been jaywalking, the woman had been speeding. Not by much, but enough to make a court case inevitable. The hospital bills were too much for my mother to pay.

My mother and I faced the judge, aware of his authority. My mother was dressed in one of her lustreless '80s real estate outfits. Crystal beads of sweat dotted her lips—evidence of her distress. My back was hunched forward. I felt tiny streaks of sweat trickle down my side.

From what I can recall, my mother had asked for enough money to take care of the hospital bills. The judge lingered over the settlement papers, his black robe resting on the edges of his desk, his gavel placed squarely before him. Then he looked up.

'Mrs Neutill, do you think this sum is worth your daughter's arm?'

'What?' she replied.

'I am asking if you think this amount is enough to not only cover the cost of medical bills but also future care in case there are long-term effects from this accident? Is this the value of your daughter's arm?'

'Sir, I do not know what you mean,' my mother said, confused. Her accent felt more discernible than ever before. The expression on her face was one I had witnessed many times. She looked lost, desperate for answers and a means of controlling the world and our future.

The judge peered down at me, his eyes narrowed to slits. He appeared both concerned and stern.

'I don't think it is. I think it's important that you think of your child's future, Mrs Neutill, don't you?'

He raised the settlement sum to an amount he deemed appropriate. Sadness and a tinge of detachment came over me.

Tears welled up in my eyes, but I was finally learning to control them. I bit my tongue and concentrated on the pain.

Years later, this would unravel in reverse. I would sit in a courtroom and have my daughterly intentions interrogated, and once again, I would force myself not to cry so I could remain composed and thereby prove that I was someone responsible, capable of caring for my mother. But in this moment, for the first time, someone was questioning how well my mother cared for me.

Under the judge's paternalistic gaze, I realized that my mother might not be the best of mothers. Suddenly, I couldn't control the tears any longer.

During this time, our lives would start shifting, in ways unbeknownst to us.

Rekha was my mother's best friend. Being my mother's friend meant a cyclical relationship of affection and anger. My mother would get mad at Rekha for reasons that were unclear, just as she would with me; she would cut off their relationship for months, sometimes a year. Then, suddenly, Rekha would call her, as if she knew enough time had passed, and my mother would no longer be angry with her.

Rekha was a Bengali woman who dyed her hair blonde and wore low cut shirts. Her lips were always painted a deep shade of burgundy, so dark I sometimes wondered if the colour was black. She was sexy and abhadra—the disreputable woman in Bengali culture, shunned and relegated to the borders of society because she wasn't pure and chaste.

We met her when I was six or seven in Venice Beach while my mother and I were strolling on the multicoloured sand. My mother loved the ocean, but she never went in the water. While she adored the way it looked, she recognized that it was an unpredictable force filled with the unknown, and that even though it appeared calm, it could turn violent any moment, just like her.

Rekha and my mother hit it off as soon as they met. Perhaps my mother liked that Rekha was different from her. Next to her, my mother was a good bhadra woman, at least from the outside. My mother didn't expose her cleavage, she wore light make-up, and she always covered her legs.

Rekha's husband, Amitava, was a fiery man. He was of medium height with a mane of jet-black hair that hung thick and wavy all the way to his shoulders. He wore thick silver jewellery—rings on every finger and chunky bracelets dotted with turquoise and coral. I was afraid of his loud voice and the force of his masculinity which he performed with bluster. He didn't seem to be afraid of anything.

Rekha was a singer, and Amitava was her manager. They lived in a large house in Orange County with beat-up Mercedes-Benzes and BMWs lining the driveway. I will never know how they afforded any of their possessions.

Rekha gave me make-up and new clothes—not hand-me-downs like my mother, all her clothes from the '70s which I would later cherish. While my arm was broken, Rekha came over with shopping bags filled with delights—stonewashed Jordache jeans; T-shirts plastered with the faces of Prince and Samantha Fox and New Kids on the Block; CDs and posters of Michael Jackson and Madonna in her lace corset and dangling pearls, which I hung on my bedroom wall. These were symbols of my cultural assimilation—my running away from Bollywood and my turn towards Hollywood; my sprinting away from my mother.

When my mother saw the things in the bags, she immediately said, 'You shouldn't spoil her. She shouldn't be wearing such sexy clothing.'

Rekha laughed. 'Oh, come on, yaar. She has had a tough time. Look at her arm. She deserves some fun.'

I was so excited to have someone stick up for me. Someone who was simply articulating that my desires were generic. That they were desires that most kids have—to be and possess all the things that make them seem 'normal'.

My mother could tell that the older I became, the more I wanted her to be like Rekha, with that veneer of liberalism that would make her appear more 'American'. Rekha was a representation of all the things my mother could be—an Indian woman who let me do American things and wasn't controlled or concerned by Indian traditions and customs.

As I grew older, I got used to the comings and goings of Amitava and Rekha. I never knew when they would disappear, nor was I aware when suddenly they'd appear, as if wanting to observe what my mother was up to. I wish I could have seen the possibility of what was to come sooner.

7

THE SUMMER AFTER MY ARM healed and my cast came off, I learned how to become popular and sexy. My teacher was Elena, my best friend. We went to a public grade school together, before my mother decided that private was preferable and enrolled me in a Christian parochial school. Given that Elena was a year older—which at that age felt like a decade—I believed that she was wiser, especially about sex. She taught me about seductive clothes and blue eyeshadow, short shorts and stonewashed jeans. She introduced me to *Purple Rain* and the wetness that Apollonia's breasts could generate in me. I didn't understand how a girl could provoke these feelings in another girl and was overcome by shame whenever images of women made my groin flutter. So, I pushed those confusing feelings aside and focused on trying to make boys like me.

Elena regularly rotated her wardrobe and gave me all the clothes that she got tired of—Guess miniskirts, sweatshirts torn at the shoulder that exposed my collarbone, suggestive in their curves. She said that one day I would be all grown up and pretty, just like her. Elena was simply cooler than me.

'This is how you should look when you're talking to a boy,' Elena said one day as she pushed her lips out to try to make them bigger and juicier. She lowered her eyes as if to give herself a demure appearance. She looked more like a puppy washed in shame, but at that age, I just wanted to mimic her appearance. I pursed my lips to try and replicate her perfect pout.

'Stop, you're doing it wrong! You look stupid,' Elena yelled. 'Rule number one: don't seem *desperate*,' she explained.

'What?' I asked.

'That's how you get people to *want* you and *be friends* with you. You have to be aloof, otherwise people will think you're weak.'

Elena was so much older than any other thirteen-year-old.

We were going to meet some boys with Elena's friend Mariana, who was two years older than her. Mariana had dark brown hair, olive skin and striking round brown eyes. Her mouth would be covered in bright red lipstick that made her appear seventeen instead of fourteen. Her wardrobe enhanced the façade of womanhood—close-fitting black leotard tops that accentuated her growing breasts, stonewashed jeans that clung tight around her ass. She stank of maturity.

Mariana had been hanging out with a guy named Eric. He was nineteen and thought she was seventeen. They had got to third base. Mariana told Elena and me that when he put his fingers inside her, she moaned, and it was a sound of consummate pleasure. She never told us whether the sound was feigned or real.

We walked over to the park down the street from Elena's house to meet Eric and his friend Diego. I held on to the perfect pout that had taken hours to earn Elena's approval.

Eric was pale, with thick black hair that he wore gelled against his scalp. His body was of a medium build. Diego, by contrast, was brown, and had forearms that were so sculpted I wanted to pet them.

Eric leaned up against his car, his arms crossed at his chest. He examined me slowly from head to toe. 'Who's *this?*' he asked.

'This is Rani, Elena's best friend,' Mariana said.

'Hi, Rani. How old are you?'

'I'm the same age as Mariana,' I responded, still concentrating on my pout as I tried to hold it in place while I spoke.

He stared at me, as if assessing whether or not I was telling the truth. I felt the pout beginning to evaporate.

'You a good girl, Rani?' he asked.

'Yeah, she is,' Elena said as she laughed. 'She's a good little Indian girl.'

'Indian?' Eric asked.

'Yeah,' I responded. 'My mom is from India.'

'That's where you get those big eyes, aye?'

'I guess,' I mumbled. I started to feel awkward, my pout more and more difficult to hold in place. Still, I tried to maintain the illusion of desirability.

When it was time for us to return to Elena's house, Eric slipped me his number.

'You know … in case you ever want to hang out.'

I called him the next day. I didn't care that Mariana was interested in him. He was the first boy to look at me with what I understood to be pure and unadulterated sexual interest. That mattered more than anything.

Eric and I began to call each other every week and my mother caught me on the phone with him more than once.

The first time I got caught, it was late at night. I had my small TV on in the background. Its slight glow shaded the room in hues of navy-blue and mustard. Moving images intermittently flickered, a strobe that simultaneously hid and exposed my growing sexual desire. Eric told me that when we next hung out, he would take off my clothes. My short Guess miniskirt. The sweatshirt I'd cut at the collar, so it hung off my shoulder and exposed my tanned, brown skin. Eric said he would take off my cotton panties and stick one, then two, then three fingers inside me. I could feel myself drip with absolute wanting. I lied to him and said I'd done it all before. That's when I heard my mother—the scuffle of her bare feet on the ceramic tiles as she walked down the hallway to enter my bedroom.

'Eric, I have to go.'

Click.

My mother appeared before me. Her nightgown was crinkled. An iron had not touched it for weeks.

'You are not allowed to talk to boys!' she yelled, as she grabbed the phone, furiously shaking the cord to remove the receiver from the wall. She threw the phone onto the carpet, and it jangled its way across the floor. When she reached for my ear, I knew the precise direction and speed at which her hand would travel through the air. At twelve, I was finally strong enough to fight back. I grabbed her wrist and turned it. As my mother winced with pain, I recalled how my Dida had ferociously pulled my mother's arm. My mother had resisted her, just as I was resisting now. She lunged forward as if to throw me across the room, and I put my hands on her shoulders to push her away. My mother grasped my hair and began to yank at it. But I was taller than she was and could easily grab a hank of her hair myself. I tugged at the strands until she shrieked. We remained locked in a cradle of enmity, sweating, gasping for air, our faces so close that I could feel her searing breath. My teeth were clenched. I started to grind them together and felt the uneven texture of my molars. I took my elbows and placed them on her breasts, shoving her away from me. She staggered from the force of my retaliation; the impact of my bones imprinted on her chest.

My mother had no idea how to respond. She must have felt the hatred beneath my skin. She must have seen it in the sweat that beaded above my lip. I was lit up like a neon sign, every part of me declaring my disdain for her. I had turned my mother's violent choreography against her, just as she had turned it against her own mother. She did not know how to mother a daughter who had learned to behave just like her, a daughter who was finally making childlike sense of the violence she had witnessed her entire life.

We stared at each other. There was nothing more to do.

'*Ami ki korbo*? What am I going to do?' My mother turned quiet after letting slip the statement, her anger and strength spent. She picked up the phone and took it to her bedroom. I slammed my bedroom door and locked it, climbed under the brown duvet cover of my single bed and thought of the ways boys could provide me with an escape from my mother, love me in all the ways she did not.

During the 1980s, abstinence-only education was the law of the land, and as an Indian woman who grew up in the '50s and '60s, my mother was never given the tools to educate a child about sex.

Besides, her approach to my budding sexuality was in no small measure informed by her colonial past. Constraints on women and their sexuality had long been a political tool of the British in India. The British claimed that they were trying to save brown women from the violence of brown men; that India was a brutal, backward place that needed to be civilized. These emergent ideologies were simply wrapped in a new package postindependence, with many women having to make a choice between a marriage and an education—but no matter what they chose, and even if they chose both, they were subject to the powers of men. In this regard, Indian men were no better than the white men who had ruled them, and Indian women were the casualties of their struggle for domination. Their lives were circumscribed, their desires were beasts to be tethered, their imagination and corporeality had to be subjugated.

While I knew that my mother was an Indian woman trying to abide by these traditions, I didn't understand that she was also attempting to make up for her own failure to abide by those traditions. Before my father—a white man twenty-five years her senior—there had been transgressions that I wasn't yet aware of, that had 'endangered the family name'.

Much of this could not be articulated by my mother. What she saw and perceived was a daughter who refused to be reined in. My mother's last resort was to care for me the way *her* mother cared for her—through a violent rendering of love.

8

WHEN I WAS VERY YOUNG, my mother would tell me stories that I did not understand, stories about a twisted family tree with sick roots and rotting fruit.

Much later in my life, others would confess our history—how my mother's and my Tapati Mashi's madness were the nexus of so much strife. When it was far too late, one of my aunts would tell me about the moments of violence my mother witnessed as a child, and how, later, my Dida had wanted to lift the family out of poverty by using my mother's beauty. But Tapati Mashi's illness was an impediment.

My mother would, sometimes, look out of the window of her bedroom, into the sunset, trying not to listen to the voices in her head. As an adult, I can only wonder if the voices she heard were the discordant sounds of the tales she wasn't allowed to tell.

There are times I play out the scenes of these forgotten stories, imagining how they unfolded.

It was the late 1950s. My mother was ten years old, my Tapati Mashi was eighteen. Rima Mashi was out of the house, maybe in college. Tapati Mashi had always been an anomaly, but her peculiarities had evolved unmistakably into mania. She had been married off at sixteen. But her husband had died. She had to return to my Dida's flat because she had nowhere else to go, and in her world, what affliction was worse than being a widow!

Historical legacies plagued Tapati Mashi. Early marriage was designed to protect women, who were considered property, from becoming *damaged* property. Nationalism insisted that the vulnerability of a woman threatened the masculine contours of family and country—a widowed woman was nothing more than a symbol of castration.

Only now do I understand that Tapati Mashi's status as a widow, and my own mother's widowhood, magnified the precarity of their condition. Without men, they were unable to play their roles as protectors of national identity, the worth of their bodies and minds ruined.

How could anyone not go mad in the face of this?

Later in life, I would hear rumours that Tapati Mashi had been threatened by a man in the neighbourhood. Her widowhood and the threat she confronted finally derailed her; they denied her a foothold in reality. She could not stand without swaying. Her mind fluttered about as she searched for a solid, flat line. My mother peered around the corner to see her sister frantically pulling her hair.

One day, matters came to a boil. My Dadu reached for Tapati Mashi's wrist. He pulled her down the hallway, opened the front door, and dragged her up the stairs towards a small room on the roof. My mother quietly followed, one bare foot following the other. Once my Dadu reached the room, he took Tapati Mashi inside and slammed the door shut.

My Dida was downstairs. Her hands covered her ears.

My mother heard her sister's screams, acutely aware that what was happening was terrible. A beating to whip away my Tapati Mashi's abnormalities.

When my Dadu opened the door, the force of his blows had not magically transformed my Tapati Mashi into what everyone wanted to see—an ordinary young woman. Instead, Tapati Mashi clutched a piece of cloth in her hand, a shred from her white sari. She crushed the cloth into a tight ball and shoved it into her mouth. Cotton flowered around her lips.

My mother crawled down the stairs and snuck into my Dida's flat, all the way to the small closet in a corner. She heard the caws of blue-black crows that sat on the roof of the building next door. She put her back to the wall and slid down until she reached the floor, hoping she might become invisible.

Seven years after hearing her sister's cries, my mother was tasked with saving the family from poverty.

My Dida coaxed my mother to lure in a boy named Sunil, the son of a wealthy zamindar, with her body. When my Rima Mashi found out, she was horrified. Her shock, her shame, drew my Dida's fury.

My mind conjures up the scene.

My Dida stood by her bedroom doorway, her hands in tight fists. '*Beriye jao bari theke!* Get out of my house!' she yelled. The photos of Shirdi Sai Baba and Ma Durga, on the altar next to her bed, shivered.

'Ma! She can't be spending time alone with that boy!' Rima Mashi yelled back. 'What will the neighbours think? God forbid, what if she gets pregnant?'

'I know what I am doing!' my Dida shouted.

'*Tumi pagol*! You're crazy. You are ruining our name! We already have to deal with Tapati!' Rima Mashi's voice turned shrill, exasperated at my Dida's seemingly irrational beliefs.

'This is *my* house,' my Dida retorted. 'She is *my* child. If I am not worried about her behaviour, you shouldn't be either. If you don't like it, I repeat, get out!'

Rima Mashi was right. My Dida was making decisions that were perilous. Yet, my Dida's response was to push her daughter away.

What kind of resentments burrowed into my aunt's psyche, knowing that my grandmother preferred one daughter above the rest? My mother's light skin and beauty, which my Dida believed to be profitable assets, made this daughter more valuable than any of her other children. Animus must've planted its seeds in my Rima Mashi's mind. Anger must've seeped into her skin, placed on a burner, waiting to boil.

The building my mother and aunts lived in was my Dida's inheritance—the last remnant of her father's wealth. My Dida's stories often involved her tumultuous past. She told me that my great-grandfather had been a wealthy industrialist from Barisal, East Bengal, and had flourished under British rule. My Dida's childhood had been filled with luxury—toys, rich food, delectable morsels of gurer-sondesh. When my Dida's father died at forty, he left his business to his four sons. There arose the predictable battle that comes from any inheritance so large. As often happens, at the end of it, little was gained monetarily by anyone at all.

My Dadu was a lawyer. His law degree should have provided them with a comfortable level of wealth. Appetizing food should have lined their kitchen table; gold jewellery should have filled their safe; the dark soot that formed on the edges of the building and that slowly began to creep across the mustard-coloured surface should have been cleaned. But my grandfather was what my Dida called 'a do-gooder'. He met with clients who didn't have money and never aspired to accumulate wealth. He wanted peace of mind and was willing to give up peace at home to gain the strength that comes from relinquishing all earthly belongings. When he eventually fled the insanity of the women in his family and became a monk, he achieved the accord he had so desired. I wonder if he ever questioned what role he'd played in their madness.

'*Tumi merudondo heen!*' my Dida would yell at him. 'You are spineless!'

I imagine he did not cower. 'Ask your brother for money,' he would calmly respond.

And she did ask her brother.

My Dida's gender rendered her powerless. She could not work, given the world she belonged to. Her only job was to be a mother. Since most of my Dida's six daughters had been married off, except for my Rima Mashi, dowry expenses had further depleted the family's savings. She begged her eldest brother for money to educate my mother. He obliged and offered to fund my mother's degree at Jadavpur University.

My Dida hoped that Sunil would marry my radiant mother and save them from a life of poverty. The assurance offered by marriage was sex. My Dida believed that Sunil would be so sexually enthralled by my mother, so bewitched by her, that he would marry her. Such was the power Dida invested in my mother's beauty.

The night before my mother was to meet Sunil's parents, Rima Mashi had seen them. My mother and Sunil were on the ground floor, alone. They were sweating, my mother's sari uncoiled across a small bed.

'Do you love me?' my mother asked Sunil.

'Of course,' Sunil responded as he rose up and moved away from her to dress.

'Your family is coming to meet me tomorrow, yes?' my mother replied, her voice filled with anticipation.

'Yes, yes, tomorrow. I will be there. I promise.'

The next day, my mother wore a solid black sari with a white and red paisley border, the edges stitched in gold thread. She entered the living room where Sunil's parents waited, walking slowly, patiently, barely breathing for fear they might not like her.

Sunil's parents were already filled with the tales that fluttered about the neighbourhood. They had heard of my mother's beauty—but also of my aunt Tapati's slow slip from sanity. Not even my mother's mesmerizing eyes could undo the misfortune of madness in a family. They also knew about the illicit meetings between my mother and their son, of course. But my mother did not know that they knew.

'Nomoshkar,' my mother said.

'Ha,' Sunil's mother responded, dismissively.

Sunil's father barely looked at my mother, as if his gaze might betray his keen interest in this girl who had been meeting his only son.

'We have heard that your other daughter, Tapati, has some issues,' Sunil's mother said, as she looked at my Dida, who sat in the corner of the room, bracing herself against the armchair.

'She is fine, I assure you,' my Dida responded hastily.

'That is not what we have been hearing. We have heard that she visited Dr Banerjee and he diagnosed her with some sort of mather-dosh—mental issue.'

'Na, na,' my Dida said, decisively, as if the confidence in her tone could make everyone change their views.

'Well, the rumours are there. We do not want our son entering a family plagued with these sorts of issues.'

'Then why did you come here?' my mother asked.

'We wanted to see the woman our son has been cavorting with and ask that it stop,' Sunil's mother snapped.

How did my mother feel? Trapped by the curse of madness? Unable to move up in society without respect and financial security? Scared to name and voice her afflictions? How did she feel about Sunil? Did she love him? Or was she only following her mother's orders?

I see her looking down at her sari, the gold and paisley border, the solid black cloth. She searches for an explanation for what is happening. She finds one. *I shouldn't have worn black*, she thinks. *Black is bad luck*.

My mother's inability to please my Dida by marrying Sunil devastated her. She needed to bring my Dida financial welfare, and her beauty was the only means she had to do so. Soon after Sunil abandoned her, she began an affair with a wealthy, married Indian man. He offered to pay for her to move to England to go to beauty school. I know this because almost sixty years after my mother's indiscretion, his son reached out to tell the story. His father offered to send my mother to England so she would no longer be a temptation to him. My Dida encouraged my mother to abandon college and travel to Great Britain, a country my Dida, of course, adored.

My Dida's colonized mind envisioned streets that glimmered, and porcelain faces with rosy cheeks, blue eyes and pink lips. An Englishman for my mother. Dida imagined rows of mansions marked with history. She forgot that her own country had a longer, richer history. For my Dida, her culture was irrelevant. England was the crown jewel, even if its gems were stolen.

But in London, my mother fell in love with another Indian boy. She was renting a room from an Indian couple in Southall—that suburb of West London primarily occupied by South Asians. She paid rent with her earnings at a salon and walked miles to get to work each day. She was nineteen years old. I don't know exactly how she met Anil, but I know that he was the love of her life. She told me many times.

'He could have been your father,' she often said, when I was so young that my child's mind couldn't comprehend what she meant.

I dreamed that their encounter was romantic, but also filled with heartbreak, loss and grief. Sexual entanglement never crossed my mind. Even as I grew older, I couldn't admit that my mother had had sex before marriage. If I did, I would have had to see that my sexuality—and her response to it—was shaped by hers. She didn't want me to repeat her mistakes—or what she now perceived to be mistakes.

There were insurmountable differences between Anil and my mother. She was Bengali; he was Sindhi. She was a Brahmin. He was not. During the Partition of India, Sindhis had been displaced as India was sliced into two nations—Pakistan and India—and Brahmins had always looked down on Sindhis. While my Dida never spoke about her precise caste, I realized, as I grew older and learned about the violence and inequity of the caste system, that my Dida's silence, too, was a form of privilege.

My mother's caste and ethnicity were open wounds of resentment. Anil's parents would never approve of a woman who carried a history of prejudice against them. Possibly, they even knew about my mother's past and my Tapati Mashi's madness.

My mother told me about Anil's ultimate rejection of her numerous times. The trauma of his repudiation must have haunted her because she remembered everything, including what she had worn that day. She vividly and repeatedly narrated the story in such detail that I recall the moment as if it had happened to me.

'Do you love me?' my mother asked Anil. The question had become a mantra for my mother.

She was lying on Anil's bed in his small flat. It was winter. The smell of tandoori chicken and freshly made roti wafted in through a slim crack in the windows. My mother wore a silk sari covered with bright pink, red and yellow flowers. She must have been a splash of colour against the dreary dampness of London.

'Yes, of course, I love you,' Anil responded.

My mother was perspiring.

There was a knock at his door.

'Who is that?' my mother asked.

Anil said he didn't know.

My mother watched as he got up from his place beside her. Her question turned into another one: Does he *really* love me? She kept watching as Anil walked towards the door.

'Who is it?' he asked.

A young woman's voice replied in Sindhi.

'One minute, Radhika,' he said. He rushed back to my mother.

'You have to hide. My sister can't see you,' he said, confused as to how or where to stow my mother. A body that had just been a source of pleasure was now an inconvenience. Evidence.

My mother felt him grab her arm and drag her to the back door, his grip tight around her forearm, her flesh now crinkled, not smooth from the sweat of their sexual encounter. When he opened the door, he forgot that she was only in her colourful silk sari, her abdomen exposed, her arms bare. He pushed her into the cold, ignoring that this attempt at hiding her—the cold air on her naked skin—might be too much for her to bear.

After my father's death, Anil would visit us from London. I'd ask him about his city, the double-decker red buses and the soldiers in puffy black hats that stood stoic in front of Buckingham Palace. He'd sit on our burgundy velvet chair in our living room and answer my questions. He'd tell me how he could have been my father. That if things had worked out the way he had wanted, he would have been there to raise me.

I pictured him in our lives from the beginning and saw a father that wasn't just a voice etched on magnetic tape that lived in our media console. He would have moved us to London, the city my Dida cherished. He would have kept my mother warm and held her on nights when her mind scrambled and ghosts plagued her. He would have saved us from serial killers and kept us financially afloat.

Anil kept visiting us when I was four, five and six years old.

Until, one day, I never saw him again.

My Dida and my mother broke the rules—rules I had come to experience firsthand, and rules I had learned from books in graduate school. These rules dictated how women should act and exist. They demanded that women be chaste and educated; that they eschew sex before marriage because promiscuity made them dangerous and dirty.

My aunts' and Dida's story do not exist in a vacuum. Much has been said about the physical and economic costs of colonialism. More can be said about the psychological impact as well. What does it mean to not be full, to be constantly lacking, as someone who is colonized? How does one live a life if one is forever chasing an intangible idea, a lie peddled by the 'master'? My work as an academic obsessively circled these questions. I wrote for hours, pondering over whether the reality of the violence that was unleashed during Partition—the fact that people who looked like one another, lived amongst one another, turned against each other in a flash—was really a hostility against the self, a buried self-hatred. I pondered how much of the violence and responsibility fell upon women, their bodies and minds, their pasts and futures. I thought about how women were treated like the newly designed cartography of India: fragmented, cut, divided and abandoned.

Within my own family, I pined to know if the self-hatred had caused divisions in the minds and bodies of women; if the mandate to be like the colonizer meant that they were lesser than, abject, swivelling through their own psyche like vermin.

9

WHEN THE TIME CAME FOR me to enter the seventh grade, two things were apparent—my mother had spent our inheritance travelling the world and we could no longer afford private school. The former was more concerning to me, while the latter was terrifying to my mother. Pasadena might have had wonderful, wealthy neighbourhoods and the greatest private schools, but its public school system was suffering, where de facto segregation had existed until 1970. When action was finally taken to desegregate the system, upper- and middle-class white folks pulled their kids out and placed them in private schools. Pasadena public schools were notorious for being 'bad' and a new virus was infecting young girls across the nation—teenage pregnancy.

My mother came to believe that attending a 'low risk' school would prevent me from being infected. Our neighbouring town of Arcadia had better public schools and my mother was desperate to gain access to them. She was not alone in this regard; plenty of families with insufficient cash were finding innovative ways to get their children into 'low risk' environments, which really meant schools devoid of Black and brown students. My mother had absorbed this racism, as so many Asian immigrants do. Anti-Blackness was deeply seeded in the soil of the United States; it was the backbone that kept the top of American society white even as people of colour tried to climb their way up. Asian immigrants were used by white people as a tool—the so-called 'model minority'; a myth that fostered racism against Black people and created conflict between groups of colour in order to maintain white supremacy.

As the real estate market slowed down, my mother had more time to be worried and angry with me, more time to watch TV and more time to find out about the atrocities that talk show hosts like Oprah Winfrey, Phil Donahue and Sally Jessy Raphael loved to talk about. Oprah became my mother's best friend. Most afternoons, at 3 or 4 p.m., she sat in front of the TV on our yellow velvet sofa in the living room, sipping a cup of gorom cha and snacking on jhal-muri. She leaned in towards the glowing screen to absorb Oprah's presence. Her nose took in the sting of mustard oil with each bite, her ears the sound of Oprah's every knowledgeable word about societal ills. From *The Oprah Winfrey Show*, she learned that I was in serious danger of becoming pregnant and would need to be vigilantly monitored. The only inoculation against this malady was to attend a school in Arcadia.

It wasn't too hard for my mother to find a family that required only a bit of cash to let us use their address to attend a neighbouring school that was considered better than the public schools in Pasadena. That's how, at twelve years of age, I ended up at Dana Middle School in Arcadia for three whole months.

I started my semester at Dana Middle School, determined to use all the lessons Elena and movies like *Heathers* had taught me that summer. I had one goal—to become popular. I was determined to break the cycle of ostracization I had suffered at my former school. Being popular was a strategic process—find a girl, an easy target; make up stories about her; mobilize a group; prank call her and make her cry; embarrass her and tell yourself she deserves the abuse.

My first victim was Lola. She had also gone to my parochial school, and there, she had been popular. She had never struggled as I had. No one made fun of the smells in her house or the gods that decorated her walls. When I was included by the blonde, blue-eyed girls at my old school, Lola had acted like my friend. Whenever the popular girls remembered how distinct I was from them, she kept her distance.

I hated her. I resented how seamlessly she blended in with the admired crowd. How her whiteness made her the same as those girls. That she didn't have an Indian mother who set her apart. Lola was pretty—prettier than me—skinny, with long, light brown hair and blue eyes that shone like glass. It seemed to me that her bright white smile sprayed pixie dust into the air, a magical powder to make people desire her. Boys gawked as she walked up and down the school's hallways. Girls in the grade above studied her with approval. Jealousy dripped from my eyeballs when I looked at her. Elena had, over time, trained me to be mean, and I finally had the tools to destroy Lola.

Lola's mother had been the one to tell mine about how to get around school district restrictions. She was helpful, and in return, I made her daughter's life miserable. I made Lola pay for what wasn't her fault—that she was more coveted than me—by uttering a few false statements.

'She hates you, you know?' I told one of our classmates, who was being instructed by an older girl on how to be popular.

'What do you mean?'

'Well, Lola was talking about the outfit you were wearing the other day. She just said that it was ugly.'

'What?' Her nostrils flared.

So very little was required to make this classmate believe that Lola was a mean girl. One lie, no verification necessary, and the rumours began—that she was vicious; that she was undeserving of the approving looks from older girls and the stares from boys.

We began to prank call Lola. In her weakened state, she faded into the background. The older girls in school started to talk to me between classes instead of her. We continued our harassment to make Lola pay for all the insults and catty comments she had never made.

Before long, Lola's mother began to see how miserable her daughter was. When she'd pick up the phone, she would hear the heavy breathing or the whispers of, 'Lola, you're such a bitch, hehehe.'

Lola knew I was jealous and resentful and that the class was happy to elevate me to the position of a ringleader. She knew that I was the one who had got the other girls to turn on her. As soon as my role in her misery became clear, Lola's mother went straight to the principal to tell him that my mother was breaking the law by circumventing the system and that she had not kept her daughter within the proper school boundaries. I wonder if it would have been as easy to blame me if my mother was wealthy and white. In any case, Lola's mom took the most appropriate revenge possible—she got me expelled.

My expulsion proved my mother right. I was an atrocious child with a vile tongue. She, in turn, began to tell people that I was too much to handle. Not even the right school could fix me.

I would sometimes find my mother on the edge of her bed, looking out of those large sliding glass doors at LA's smog-ridden skyline, asking the air or her imaginary friends why she deserved such a terrible child. Answers weren't forthcoming. The ghosts of her past were slowly colonizing her mind;

hallucinations were taking over. With each passing year, she wriggled towards madness.

The only way my mother could discipline me was by telling me I was a bad girl. Each time she did, I felt the blow of her words; they punctured my skull and whipped my body. A sorrow formed in some central place in me. It was a sadness that made a comfortable home in my core and would never go away. I didn't know that soon I would be displaced; I'd be sent far away from home.

WINTER 2015
RETURNING

IT FEELS LIKE WE SPEND hours in the ambulance, meandering the roads of Kolkata, my mother's hand in mine, her gaze on me. Her skin feels so thin, as if it will tear open from the slightest scratch. I shift my gaze and look out the window. Cars beep along, with the ambulance's siren like a cacophonous jazz fugue. As I watch the vehicles thread around each other, I recall the many times my mother yelled at me and said, 'You were such a bad child. What was I supposed to do with you?'

At this moment, I think she is right.

Five years before, in 2010, my mother's health had taken a turn for the worse. I had not spoken to her for two years, during which time she had been living in Kolkata. My Rima Mashi had called me to tell me that my mother had suffered a ruptured aneurysm and was being rushed into brain surgery.

When I arrived, she was bedridden, and my Rima Mashi was caring for her.

Where once my mother's memory had been as sharp as a shiv—she remembered phone numbers like a human Rolodex, meticulously stored past events in her mind and threw memories of my bad behaviour at me like grenades—now, she couldn't remember anything. Now, she was broken. I wanted to cradle her and stroke her hair to ease her scrambled mind. Love radiated from my fingertips.

I flew my mother back to the United States, where I became helpless in the face of her deteriorating mental facilities. She had never arranged to give me any kind of authority to care for her, because why would she have ever thought to do so? In India, siblings are charged with their parents' well-being simply because they are kin. And even if she had thought to formally assign me power as a caregiver, I doubt she would have been able to go through with it. My mother couldn't imagine a life in which she didn't have autonomy. She needed the ability to do as she pleased; it was the only thing that gave her the illusion of control.

After my mother's aneurysm, she developed dementia and refused to take any of the medications her doctor prescribed. She started having small seizures that worsened her memory loss. She couldn't remember to pay her bills. When I discovered she had begun calling temples and gurus and offering them her life's savings, I sat in my kitchen biting my lower lip. My phone sat in front of me. I stared at it, frantically wondering who I could call to ask for help. I wished I believed in astrology like my mother did, or gurus, so that someone would tell me what the best course of action was. The longer I sat there, the more I realized what I needed to do was the thing I dreaded the most.

I applied to the Los Angeles County Court to become her conservator—essentially, her legal guardian. Suddenly, at thirty-two, I was sitting in front of a judge who carefully slid his glasses up his nose, securing them against his face, so he could peer down at me and determine if I was well-intentioned enough, stable enough and competent enough to be my mother's custodian. I anxiously waited for him to slam his gavel down from his seat of power and confirm that I was a good daughter, worthy of taking care of my mother.

These legal affairs made no sense to the woman who birthed me. After all, where she came from, care was about custom and kinship and an inheritance of duty (and my mother liked reminding me that, as her daughter, I hadn't done enough). In California, care for a parent took the form of reading and signing court documents and learning terms like 'conservator of the estate' and 'conservator of the person'.

I was appointed conservatorship of my mother's estate by the court; I had to care for and protect her finances. But, like many ageing parents, my mother didn't believe that anything was wrong with her. Despite what the doctors told her, she couldn't comprehend that she was ill, that the conservatorship was in her best interest. Instead, she believed I was seeking revenge for her past violence and abandonment. I always wondered if she was partly right, if I was glad my mother finally knew what it was like to be stripped of all agency.

Around the time I was given charge of caring for my mother's finances, Amitava, who had woven in and out of our lives during my childhood, reappeared. I had not heard of him or his wife Rekha—my mother's best friend—for years. At some point, Rekha had probably called my mother, or my mother had called her. But the details escape me.

My mother told Amitava about the conservatorship, perhaps because she believed I was trying to hurt her. Amitava didn't challenge the belief or the idea that she had to end this 'conservatorship bullshit'.

I started feeling frightened each time Amitava called. My brain throbbed with confusion. My cellphone trembled in my hand.

But I am my mother's daughter. I did not back down.

Five years later, my mother is near death. I have not done my job as her guardian.

As we zigzag through the streets of Kolkata, I have yet to comprehend the dynamics that have led my mother and me to this moment—with the rickety plank of wood my mother is lying on, the old, rusted oxygen tank beside her, and the tears that leak from my eyes.

But soon, I will.

10

AFTER MY EXPULSION FROM SCHOOL, my mother railed against me and avoided me by turns. Often, she would spend hours in her bedroom on the phone. One day, I put my ear against her bedroom door and tried to discern her muffled sentences. When she finally came out, she pushed me into the hallway and yelled, 'Pack your things!'

My mother walked to one of our two bathrooms—the one with his-and-her sinks designed for two people to brush their teeth at the same time. My mother and I may have been a couple, but not the kind these bathrooms were designed for. She grabbed my toothpaste and toothbrush and shoved them into my hand. '*Taratari kara*! Be quick!'

I walked silently to my room to grab a few pieces of clothing from my closet, a bra and underwear from my dresser. My hands were shaking as I slipped these inside a thin plastic bag and threw my toothbrush and toothpaste on top. A tiny bit of aqua blue toothpaste gel smeared against my white underwear; a waft of spearmint travelled to my nose. I stared down at my things, wonderstruck and slowly realizing that maybe my mother was kicking me out of the house. I grabbed a fistful of make-up. Even if my mother was getting rid of me and dropping me off at some unknown location, I wanted to look pretty.

I was too scared to ask where we were going.

'*Theek ache*, that's enough for now.'

She drove me to Mrs Clark's house.

Mrs Clark was the mother of a classmate of mine—Heather. Heather was the most popular girl in ninth grade at Dana

Middle School. Her long, thick, wheat-coloured hair looked like a massive golden sheath of woven cloth. She manifested white-girl-perfection. She styled her bangs each day so that they stuck up six inches high. It was a late '80s hair sculpture of pure accomplishment. My hair couldn't hold that regal posture. My hair was an '80s failure. Heather had befriended me before my fall from the ranks of the high queens. Once I'd been expelled, she stopped answering my phone calls or inviting me over to learn how to make my hair a masterpiece.

Mrs Clark fostered children, including a boy who was physically challenged. I was never able to really look at him. I wanted to be what was considered 'normal', and he was a painful reminder that I wasn't 'normal' either. Back then, being 'normal' for me meant being white, pretty, thin and able-bodied, and my mother's rage, ethnicity and accent made me anything but.

When I was younger, my mother's beauty had made up for all the ways that I was not like the children I went to school with. I was bewitched by her black hair, her peaked cheekbones and her cherry lips. She had a face shaped like a peach. But she had morphed into something else since then. Rage had distorted her face, and her attention to her clothing felt careless. I'd realize later that she was still beautiful. It was my perception of beauty that had changed, a by-product of my hatred for my mother and my desire to look like the popular white girls. I had become like my Dida. My mind had been colonized.

We sat in Heather's driveway for a moment. My mother's face grew pale. I felt that she couldn't breathe—whether from sadness or anger, I couldn't tell, the two emotions intertwining inside of her like a Mobius strip.

'You are staying here. See if another mother is better than me!'

My mother walked me to the entrance and knocked to announce our arrival. When Mrs Clark opened the door, my mother pushed me inside.

'Here she is,' my mother said. 'I hope you can help train her to be a good girl.' She didn't say anything else. Instead, she scurried back to her car and did not look at me as she drove away. Mrs Clark scowled, Heather right behind her on the wooden staircase that led to her room, where bottles of Aqua Net and piles of blue eyeshadow and bright pink lipstick sat on her dresser. It was clear my mother had reported me as a terrible child in need of some serious discipline. I knew from Heather's expression that I was no longer someone to coach in popularity. I was a burden.

'Heather, take her bag to your room,' Mrs Clark instructed.

I looked down at my tiny plastic bag filled with just a few days of clothes and some toiletries, the smear of blue toothpaste on my white underwear now congealed. I no longer smelled anything minty.

'You. You come with me,' Mrs Clark directed.

The curtains in her house hung heavy, and muted sunlight veined each room, illuminating the disorder. Everything felt dark, dreary and filled with dust. I sensed a sneeze coming on and concentrated on tightening the muscles inside of my nose. I didn't want to make a sound.

I followed Mrs Clark to the kitchen and positioned myself on an uncomfortable chair. Apprehension took hold of me as I waited to be yelled at. Part of me had hoped that Mrs Clark would actually *like* me. Maybe she would think I was a normal kid, with normal kid-turned-teenager thoughts and desires. Maybe she wouldn't yell at me for talking to boys. Maybe she'd tell people I was not a difficult child. But when I saw the look on Mrs Clark's face, I knew the scenario I longed for was only a fantasy.

'This is my house, and you'll do what I tell you. I expect you to behave while you stay with me, do you hear me?'

'Yes,' I responded meekly.

All I could think was: *Where will I go from here? Maybe I can still be popular?* I felt a heavy pressure in my body, against my head. During my time at Mrs Clark's house, everything I'd do would be wrong.

One morning, hunger woke me. My stomach growled, vibrating through me like a whale singing in the ocean. I searched the house for signs of movement. No one had woken from their slumber but me. I went to the kitchen. There was a cake stand on the counter, a store-bought crumb cake on top and a glass dome to close it away. I lifted the cloche and felt its smoothness against my hand; it was heavy and unwieldy. I gently placed it on the counter to ensure that the glass didn't clink-clank or make a thud. I cut the tiniest sliver, so miniscule I thought no one would notice. I just wanted a bite of the cake to feed the whale crooning inside of me. I wanted to feel the rough edges of that cake in my mouth, dissolve the crumbs with my saliva, make them disappear into my stomach, leaving the aftertaste of sugar on my tongue.

Later in the day, I found Heather and Mrs Clark in the kitchen. My eyes glazed over the crumb cake that was still enveloped in smooth glass.

Mrs Clark glared at me, then pointed. 'Did you have some of that?'

I looked down at the floor with guilt. I had taken just a tiny bit. How did she know?

'I did. I'm sorry. I was just hungry and everyone was asleep.'

'Don't you ever take anything from this house without asking. Ever. You need to learn manners, young lady. You need to learn a lot of things.'

I never found out why Mrs Clark took me in for that week—whether my mom paid her a bit of cash or just asked her to discipline me. I imagine the transaction involved money for basic necessities and the overall arrangement appealed to Mrs Clark's desire to reform children. My mother did not call, and no one told me how long I would be staying. I didn't ask whether she would be coming back for me, or if I would become a foster child, left to travel through the system, moving from home to home.

The week I spent in Heather's home was also a lesson in humility.

'It's cold today,' I pronounced one evening, as I tried to make conversation with Heather. I wanted her to recognize my existence.

She looked at me for a brief moment as her eyes rolled up towards the indigo sky, then said, 'You really do always state the obvious.'

I still think of her when I state anything that approximates the obvious. When it's hot and I say, 'Damn, it's hot,' or when something is expensive and I note that it is, I recall Heather's beautiful face, her immaculate '80s hair sculpture, and a hint of shame starts to roll through me. I feel a pang of disgust for the little girl I once was.

11

'YOU NEED TO PACK,' MY mother said when she picked me up from my weeklong stay at Mrs Clark's house. The interior of the car was in disarray—invoices from travel agencies, rusty coins in the cracks of the car seats, bottles of water and boxes of Medjool dates on the floor, a tiny crystal Ganesh glued to the dashboard to keep us from getting into a car accident. Our home had begun to look more and more like this as well, cluttered with bottles of vitamins, piles of folders with unpaid bills, flyers for houses that had not sold, empty chequebooks. The flowered wallpaper in the kitchen was starting to peel off.

'We are going to visit your Dida for a few weeks,' my mother said.

'What about school? Aren't you going to find me a new school?'

That summer, I had been hanging out with Elena, and she had introduced me to Eric. The last thing in the world that I wanted to do was go to India, because my attachment to all things American had grown as strong as my sexual desires. I resented our time in my mother's homeland, how I had nothing to do, no boys to talk to, only a few V.C. Andrews novels to occupy my time.

'I called all the schools in the area. None of them want you.'

I didn't question the veracity of my mother's statement. I *was* a bad girl. Of course nobody wanted me.

I packed shirts, shorts and tank tops—anything to expose my skin and make me feel desirable. I also packed some of my mother's old clothing, a few tattered salwar kameezes. I had once revelled in wearing thick silver anklets that rang with every footstep; I had loved the colourful, flowing dupattas I could wear around my neck and shoulders; I had adored the chromatic display of saris that lined my mother's long closet. Now I found these items old-fashioned—this notion of having to cover up one's body. We lived in Los Angeles and we travelled often to Kolkata. Nothing about the climate of those two places ever screamed *wear more clothing*.

And yet, saris exposed one of the most erotic parts of the body—the abdomen. At that age, I could not comprehend the contradiction. Why did a woman's sexuality need to be veiled and seen at the same time?

I just wanted to be American and spray my hair with Aqua Net, wear Guess jeans and fit in with the blue-eyed girls at school. I wanted Sara Lee pies and donuts, Coca-Cola and evenly paved concrete roads where shiny cars drove in between the lines. I wanted to be a copy of the American teenagers I saw in films like *Pretty in Pink* and *Valley Girl*. I didn't want a crazy mother who made me go to a country that I considered un-American.

Here I was, so close to having something more beautiful, to being someone worth loving—and my mother was dragging me away, reminding me: I was her daughter, and nobody wanted me.

On our flight to Kolkata, just as we were placing our luggage in the overhead compartments in economy, someone called to say a bomb was located somewhere on our plane.

31 January 1990: 253 passengers and 21 crew members were shepherded off the plane by slender stewardesses and airport officials dressed in black suits, walkie-talkies firmly held in their hands. We sat for over three hours in a sterile room, while dogs sniffed the airbus, searching for explosives. The seats were uncomfortable and there was nowhere to lie down but on the rough carpeted floor. It should have been a sign, some sort of warning, that my life was going to change. Instead, I was dreaming about losing my virginity.

I was reading a Sidney Sheldon novel, slurping up the bad sexual innuendoes. I imagined having sex with Eric, the first boy to want me in all the ways I wanted to be wanted. I outlined the details of what he might do—I pictured him and his penis, and when I imagined him as he put it inside me, a warmth ran up my clitoris into my vagina. My body acted without my permission. I squeezed my legs together to try to make the feeling stop. That only made my vagina feel warmer, made the pulsations accelerate. The room zoomed out. I was at the end of some involuntary masturbation tunnel. It felt as if my clitoris had expanded, making my body roll in small waves, until I orgasmed without touching myself at an airport in front of 253 passengers, not one of whom noticed.

The bomb delayed our trip to Kolkata. We spent a day in Tokyo and a few days in Singapore, all paid for by the airline. My mother had us wander the streets together, eat crabs drenched in chilli and black bean sauce, and visit the outdoor food courts that served Malaysian cuisine—spicy, creamy coconut noodle soups with jumbo prawns, their heads, eyes and barbed legs still attached.

She bought me clothes from street vendors.

'This. This will look nice on you,' she said as she rummaged through T-shirts and jeans.

I was so excited by my new outfits. I imagined wearing them at a different school in Pasadena where I would make new friends and forget about Lola and my expulsion.

Those days were a dreamy interlude between departure and arrival. We didn't fight—a respite from the turmoil between us. Part of me pined for the times when my love for my mother was unbearable, the times when she was focused only on me. I knew that when we finally reached my Dida's flat, our ceasefire would end.

So much of me still believes that I was a difficult child and that my mother did the best she could. But I sometimes ask myself if my life would have turned out any differently if I had been a 'good' adolescent. Would I have been able to care for my mother and quiet her mind that rumbled from all she had been through? Would I have flourished into a well-mannered woman like the others I knew? Or would there still have been violence? Would my mother still have gone mad? Caring friends have said I didn't have a choice, that I was just trying to survive. But I always come back to the same nasty thought—I was unlovable.

It was winter in Kolkata, but a small bit of hot steam hit my face as the plane doors opened. Kolkata was never embarrassed to make its presence known. It was a metropolis that shook from the force of four million bodies. When you drove from the airport to the city, the smell of cow dung and smoke hung in the air. I wrinkled up my nose as we passed a maze of houses, their walls covered in manure to insulate.

Clotheslines stretched across roads and rooftops, tattered kurtas and saris hanging from them. Bird shit was splattered all over the sidewalks. Skinny street dogs prowled on every corner.

Cows lingered about, their lower jaws constantly moving in circles as they ate. Little naked children ran around the streets, their mothers watching. Cars beeped. So many cars, beeping, beeping. They spoke to each other—loudly and invasively, twenty-four hours a day. They had a way of manoeuvring through a chaotic landscape that made complete sense and no sense at all. I didn't understand their language.

My mother and I arrived at my Dida's flat. She must have heard the scrape of our large suitcases as we climbed up the steep burgundy staircase and the tired thump of plastic wheels on cement landing. She was waiting for us. Her arm held the front door wide open but her expression was blank. Sometimes, it carried a tinge of defeat—as if she were submitting to the forces of a family she did not want to be a part of anymore.

12

WHEN I WOKE UP THE morning after our arrival, my body felt pummelled from days of travelling and the shifts in time zones. I took in my surroundings. A baby blue mosquito net hung suspended from each corner of the room and cascaded around me, its edges drawn in dust and dirt. The floor of the bedroom was a burgundy concrete; a built-in bookcase with glass-panelled doors lined the wall in front of me. On one of the shelves, the Mahabharata, the Ramayana, the Bible and *Gone with the Wind*—all in English, a language my Dida could not read. The rest of the shelves were barren. A walnut armoire rested to my left, and a heavy steel safe to my right. Photos of Durga and Saraswati sat on top of the safe.

I heard my Dida and mother speaking Bengali in hushed voices.

'She doesn't know,' my mother said.

'How shall we tell her?'

'Let things take their course.'

I pushed myself out of bed, past the mosquito net, and walked into the living room. My mother and Dida stood there in their long floral nightgowns. My Dida was braless. I could see the slope of her deflated breasts and the layers of fat that bulged from her midsection.

'What's happening? What are you doing? What is happening, Ma?'

'You are going to live here with your Dida,' my mother said. 'You need discipline.'

Suddenly, I was no longer twelve years old. A maturity came over me as I tried to comprehend all that was happening, a stunning alteration of what life was going to be. I was overcome by a desperation that propelled me into some liminal space between childhood and adulthood. I cannot recall what I thought when I heard her words, but the realization hit my body before my mind. I knelt to the floor. I cupped my hands to my face and tears began to rush out of the cracks between my fingers. Then, I screamed. I shrieked so loudly the entire city must have heard my pain. I wanted the city to vibrate and stop. A metropolis that had millions of movements of its own. For a millisecond, it listened to me. I wanted Kolkata to feel my despair, to help me escape. I wanted the street dogs and cows to suspend their movements, the little children who ran around the streets splattered in bird shit to freeze into small brown cherub statues. But I knew I didn't have such magical powers; the city just moved on.

How do you even begin to describe feeling absolutely, stunningly, desperately devoid of agency? Imprisoned, and without free will. The entire city of Kolkata—the nation of India—became my jail, an uninterpretable maze I would never be able to navigate. I couldn't get out. I was twelve.

'What am I going to do here?' I asked, desperately trying to sort out what my life was going to look like.

'You are going to go to school here,' my mother yelled back. 'I can't deal with you anymore!'

I understood. I would live in Kolkata, go to school in Kolkata, live with my Dida in Kolkata.

And here I had thought I was only going to be in the city for two weeks.

My Dida had mothered seven daughters and now she was going to parent me. She had raised my mother to be a 'bad girl' because she believed my mother's beauty would save her. Now she was going to raise a child who *was* a bad girl—only one she had not nurtured or encouraged that way; a child who was light-skinned, but not light enough.

I wanted to lift myself off the floor and strike my mother, but the knowledge that there was nothing I could do froze my muscles. My bones crumbled into a powdery mess. I wanted the dry California sunshine, the warm evenings with hints of Santa Ana winds and smog-riddled sunsets. I wanted to soak myself in our warm jacuzzi and watch night fall with spectacular streaks of colour over the Los Angeles skyline. I wanted to go to an American school and befriend girls who could guide me to being prom queen. I thought of my bedroom, the blue phone that brought to me the voices of the those I wanted to be, the boys who wanted to take me in all the ways I imagined and desired. I wanted to sink my feet into my thick bedroom carpet and look through my long closet lined with hand-me-downs from Elena, clothes that bared my skin. In Kolkata, my clothes would have to cover my body to shield me from the hands and eyes of lecherous men.

I begged. 'Please, Ma. Please don't do this. I will be better, I promise. I will do whatever you tell me to do, just please take me home!'

'It has been decided. Here, you won't get into trouble.'

Each swallow I took to breathe and remain alive felt as if someone were pulling my oesophagus apart. I screamed again in an effort to make the city stop, but my mother knelt to the floor and put her hand over my mouth. Her palm tasted like salt. It felt like it would melt across my face from the heat of her anger. I tried to manoeuvre my face away so I could be heard. It was such a struggle to be heard.

I put my body back together and crawled to the bedroom. I raised the baby blue mosquito net and sank upon the hard mattress. I heard my Dida's bare feet shuffling to her room, uninterested in my pain. My lungs felt like bricks, weighing me down from the inside. I squeezed my eyes, trying to conjure a third eye, hoping it could envision a different reality and transport me to a place where none of my family existed. I begged for sleep.

When I woke up, I was still there.

I wonder now what my mother thought about as she planned our trip during my stay at Mrs Clark's house. Did she think of how she was going to live alone and needed to find a job? Maybe she was sad that she would no longer have her only child with her. Did she wonder who would look out of the windows at night in case a serial killer was coming? Maybe she was preoccupied by the possibility that she might miss me.

My mother stayed for a month. Just long enough to get me settled at my Dida's and into a new school. As she went around town talking to headmistresses, I imagined myself at one of the schools I had seen as a child. An all-girls school where students dressed in white and navy-blue uniform, their hair in the braids my mother had styled me in as a child.

But the school my mother found for me, Calcutta International School (CIS), was nothing like the one I had imagined. Open to the international community, CIS was originally built for the children of British expatriates. Most of the students were non-resident Indian kids, but the children of ambassadors and diplomats also attended.

On the day of my admissions interview, I looked around at the spacious colonial home that housed the students, a large yellow building with forest green shutters on each window. Kids my age and older sat under a covered patio with books in their hands. There were no girls in navy-blue and white uniform. Instead, the girls were dressed in their own clothing—comfortable cotton T-shirts and slacks and salwar kameezes. Boys were allowed to wear shorts and expose their legs.

The English grammar and literature teacher, Mrs Dutta, showed us around the compound. In the large backyard, students played football and cricket. Mango trees lay at the far edges, laden with green fruit shaped like commas. Tiny frogs with salmon-speckled dots leaped through the field beyond. I could hear them croaking around me. The house had two floors, with a wide walnut staircase that led to a small library filled with large wooden tables. I sat at one of them, my face still sticky and salty from days of crying. My hands rested at my sides. I pouted my way through the interview, my legs splayed open, American and unladylike.

Mrs Dutta regarded me with fierce scrutiny. She took in my mini skirt and my short-sleeved Esprit T-shirt, and the expression on her face told me that she had condemned me the moment she set eyes on me. I registered the way she took in my identity, my mixed race. I did not look like the other Bengali students, but neither did I look like the white children of ambassadors from Poland and Russia. I now suspect that my being of mixed blood offended her. The racism I had encountered had always been linked to my brown ancestry. For the first time, my whiteness was a source of prejudice. It felt strange to experience racism in another form, which came with an alternate history of difference.

'Your daughter needs to be reformed, especially her demeanour. She didn't even move her chair when the other children were trying to pass by. That is the sign of a disrespectful child,' Mrs Dutta stated, her brown-grey eyes peering at me.

'But you will take her? Let her go here?' my mother asked.

'Yes, I welcome the project. Let's see what we can do with this child.'

Over time, I began to realize the economic weight of my move. Liberalization hadn't yet taken place in India. Financial borders were stringent. A monetary summary puts into perspective just how much of a relief my move to India was for my mother. In California, attending a parochial school would cost something close to US$250 a month. But in Kolkata, before economic liberalization, my school cost only a few thousand rupees—roughly equivalent to US$20 a month. Given the dollar's strength, my clothing, books and food were all cheaper as well.

Besides, the forces of MTV and cable television had yet to filter in, and sex before marriage was culturally prohibited. India was the perfect place to cloister me. There was a double incentive to keeping me in Kolkata—birth control and financial management.

This dawned on me slowly as I grew older and began to examine my mother and our past—tiny bubbles of realization like oxygen trying to rise out of water. At the time though, all I knew was that I was an unruly child who needed to be tamed by Bengali society that believed a women needed to be virginal and dutiful and unblemished before marriage.

I still remember the day my mother left me, as if it occurred in slow-motion. She walked down the hallway of my Dida's flat towards the front door. My attention fell first on her large, navy-blue suitcase, worn from years of travel. It bore the scratches and crisscrossing lines of a life constantly lived in transit. My eyes then travelled to her face, where sadness and exhaustion had produced dark rings around the eyes, blue-grey circles that accentuated the melancholy I hoped she felt at that moment. I didn't know if I should hug her, if I should nestle my face in her hair and breathe her in as I had when I was a child. I followed her slowly, carefully, as though in a dream. I didn't know when I would see her again.

Outside of our silent moment, life was being lived in each of the floors of my Dida's building. Office workers bustled through the first floor. People chatted while they ate breakfast. Kettles whistled as each family brewed cha to go along with toast or omelettes.

My mother and I were noiseless, aside from the sound of the plastic wheels of my mother's suitcase.

My mother grasped the brass handle and pulled open the front door, stopping to look back at me. Neither of us leaned in for an embrace. We only briefly gazed at one another. And then I felt bitterness overtake me. She must have seen its shadow form on the ground beneath me. As she turned away to look at the path that led away from the house, I stepped back from her. She crossed the threshold and walked down the burgundy staircase. The door let out a sluggish clank as I closed it behind her. I walked to what had become my bedroom and lay down, holding my knees to my chest. I observed the cream wall in front of me, the powerful goddesses who hung there. Was my mother Kali or Durga? Was she the emblem of anger or the embodiment of care? And was I important enough to be conferred either?

I have never felt as desperate as I did that day—desperate to be away from my mother and be near her as well; as desperate as my mother was to know what my future held.

It felt like I had no tomorrow at all. My life would be frozen; I would forever live in the four walls of my mother's childhood bedroom and never get out.

Many children go to boarding schools, some parents send their kids to live with relatives. Was my mother really doing anything different? For so many years, I've asked myself: Did my mother really abandon me? Can I call what she did abandonment?

What I do know is that it *felt* like abandonment. It was a physical loss. My mother had made sure that she was as necessary to me as a limb. And then she had chopped herself off. Leaving me to ponder the terrifying question: who was I without my mother?

13

MISSING SO MUCH SCHOOL THROUGHOUT the years of travelling with my mother had created gaps in my knowledge. In India, I was propelled into a British curriculum vastly different from anything I had encountered in the United States—accounting, British economics, the biting violence of *Animal Farm*. I felt unintelligent around my classmates, who were already well-versed in the discourses we studied. They knew about literature and art, poetry and history—and they were only twelve or thirteen years old. They possessed good grammar and could easily deploy scholarly rhetoric. Their parents were well-off and well-educated.

I couldn't focus on *Macbeth* or *Pride and Prejudice*, which we were reading over and over in our literature class. I ignored Mrs Dutta's lessons on commas and subject-verb agreement. My desire to understand the English language was minimal compared to my desire to understand boys and their body parts. I certainly had not mastered English as thoroughly as my classmates, even if English was my first language. My grammar would forever be flawed.

'What is wrong with you? Don't you realize you'll get nowhere in life if you don't concentrate?' Mrs Dutta said repeatedly. It wasn't a question. She had a habit of comparing me to other students. 'Why don't you learn something from your classmates? See how they study?'

Mrs Ganguly, the principal and history teacher, was equally unimpressed. My Americanness was uncouth. She would glare at me with glassy eyes, her face held in a scowl. Flaps of skin hung down her face to form a wreath around her chin, the texture like rubbery folds of wattle. Every time she spoke, I imagined the rapid gurgle of a male turkey.

'Just remember, Rani. A pretty face isn't going to get you anywhere. I don't know what they do in America, but here, a good girl does her studies.'

At first, my Dida wasn't bothered that I went out after school, as long as I was home before dark. Girls who were out after dark were tawdry and shameful. It was my responsibility now to uphold the family's reputation. Despite being an American, with all the liberal sentiments Indians believed my nationality carried, I was to be a good Bengali girl.

I, however, just cared about boys. I stayed out late and went to the cinema. I arrived home when the sun had already made its sleepy descent over the squat Kolkata buildings. I waited in my bedroom for a classmate to invite me to her house, where I might encounter magical spaces called wealth, literature and art. I was learning to want to be cultured and gifted, with a philosophical mind. When I saw my Dida's body that passed gas so loudly that her farts could be heard by workers in the first-floor office below our apartment, I felt shame. I wanted to be what was considered sophisticated. I began to crave the wealthy and polished lives that all my classmates seemed to possess.

I began to fight with my Dida, as loudly as my mother and Dida had fought when I was a child. I drew myself into a likeness of my mother's existence and stood in front of my grandmother, her hot breath heaving at my face. But I never pushed her as I had pushed my mother. With her ageing body, the curved line of her back, she seemed too fragile. She might have toppled to the ground and died in front of me, her knees crashing into the hard floor. The force of my words—my screams—was enough.

I will do what I want! In those moments, I wondered if I had ever left my mother's presence, or if she had ever left mine.

Eventually, we stopped fighting. My Dida no longer had the energy to be combative. With few resources left for manic assertions of physical violence, depression took over, and as time went on, my grandmother stopped challenging my nights out. Instead, she remained still and alone in her perfectly square room, her window finally closed to the chatter of the city, as she waited to die.

The only act of violence she had left was refusing to cook.

My Dida's flat might not have been overflowing with books, but it had always been a spectacle of culinary delights. My grandmother would whip up chicken curry and mutton biriyani (the goat would be from the butcher shop across the street, where cleanly sliced goat heads and hooves cluttered the sidewalk). She'd cook my favourite dish when I was younger—muri-ghonto—fried fish heads with basmati rice, potatoes and tomatoes, bright yellow from turmeric; the smell of ginger and garlic would waft into the mouth and travel to the stomach. My Dida's food was safe from ominous parasites and the horrors of diarrhoea and vomiting that came from eating out.

Six months into my stay in Kolkata, my grandmother said: '*Ami aar ranna korbo na, Deepa korbe!*'—I am not making meals anymore, Deepa is!

My grandmother would order Deepa, a woman she had hired to cook for us for a few hundred rupees a month, from her bedroom, as she'd remain lying down. Deepa would come to the flat each afternoon, a small bag of groceries in tow, just enough to boil a pot of basmati rice and make jhinge-posto, a combination of nigella seeds, ginger and garlic paste, green or red chillies, ridge gourd, and the most important ingredient—a paste made from *papaver somniferum*, white poppy seeds.

Opium poppy. Posto—a milky, creamy, bumpy, opium-laced paste—was notorious for making you sleep. And my Dida asked Deepa to make it every day. While the sound of Deepa chopping garlic and ginger seemed to lull my grandmother with the knowledge that she would soon escape reality, it comforted me with the knowledge that I would soon be fed.

With Deepa's cooking, there was always a scarcity of food in the house. My Dida never asked Deepa to make more than the posto because she wasn't hungry anymore, her interest in life and food had waned. She wasn't aware of what a child needed because she didn't care—nothing was more important to her than retreating.

Pangs of hunger started coiling through my intestines. One night, when famishment woke me up, I tried to play chef but could barely find any food in the house. I took a small amount of phulkopi, cauliflower, from our fridge. I didn't bother to wash the ivory florets, peppered in black from sitting too long. I picked up the long lighter that lay on our stone countertop and approached the gas stove, the portable propane tank near my legs. Propane tank explosions were often in the news, and every time someone lit the gas from one of the two burners, I imagined the tank exploding, bodies ripped into jagged shapes, innards dotting the floor. I removed a pot from one of the cupboards and some soy sauce and mustard oil. I dumped half a vat of mustard oil into the pot and waited for it to sizzle—the oil needed to be piping hot, I knew this much. I threw the phulkopi in and a spray of hot oil stung my face. I covered the cauliflower in a generous amount of soy sauce. Thinking I had just mastered the art of Chinese cuisine, I scooped up my first self-made meal and began to eat. Each morsel was bitter, pungent from the nip of mustard which did not blend well with the soy sauce and had oversalted the dish. Still, I forced each piece down my throat, even though it made me wretch. The saliferous bits were still better than an aching tummy.

On most days, I went to school with nothing in my belly. I started eagerly waiting for the afternoons when, instead of Deepa's meals, I could go out to different restaurants to eat. I would sneak into my Dida's bedroom in the morning, while she slept, to steal a few twenty-rupee notes. My classmates and I would travel to the momo huts around town to eat their dumplings or search for bhel puri and kathi roll stalls. Each day I became more tolerant to the terrors of street food. My body got better and better at relishing the savoury delights of the dirty tamarind water that accompanied puchka from Vivekananda Park. I developed an adaptive immunity, an immunological memory.

If my Dida learnt that I was stealing money, she didn't seem to care. On my part, I didn't understand that cooking had been a burden to her, a responsibility that had been forced upon her hands at only twelve years of age.

I didn't realize she had fallen into an abyss from which she would never return.

Just as my Rima Mashi would come to take care of my mother over twenty years later, now Rima Mashi took care of me. My Dida's retreat from cooking led to her coming over with food.

'*Eta ki?*' What's this? Rima Mashi asked one day when she visited. She saw the scant, crusted remains of Deepa's cooking. She noticed how my Dida had begun to shrink and how hungry I looked.

Rima Mashi was divorced. Her house did not echo with the thump of children's running feet. She lived in a dreary home, where spiders with bodies the size of quarters and legs the length of fingers scurried about her walls. Every time I visited, a slight chill ran through my bones, even when the humidity outside was 100 per cent.

After she saw the remains of Deepa's posto, Rima Mashi began to come over more frequently. She would arrive at five in the evening, a tiffin carrier in tow, always in a dull cotton sari, oil permeating the thin fabric in blocks as though it were a Rothko painting. She constantly chewed paan, which stained her lips and teeth bright red; it also damaged her teeth. Her tiffin carrier was full of oily delights. My mouth watered as I waited for her to open each tier of the stainless-steel lunchbox. Her specialty was Indo-Chinese cooking, the cuisine of Tangra, Kolkata's Chinatown—chilli chicken, chicken Manchurian, chow mein noodles. She loved to fry things. She immersed each chicken and prawn cutlet in vats of ghee. She rimmed her gravy with pockets of oil that simmered and separated from the watery, curried juices that came from green peppers, garlic and tomatoes.

My Rima Mashi provided not only food, but company. At night, we watched Zee TV together. Sometimes, we sat in front of the television and took in the glow of the soap opera, *Santa Barbara*. The familiar landscape of Southern Californian bungalows and beaches made me wistful. I longed for the sandy Pacific blue coastline, and boardwalks where Ferris wheels rotated and puffy pink cotton candy was sold. We talked about the drama and intrigue, all the unimaginable calamities that could happen on screen, all the pretend stuff that soap operas promised.

Consumed with my own needs, I did not understand that Rima Mashi might eventually tire of doing the things that my mother was supposed to be responsible for—feeding me, caring for me. I missed perceiving the acrimony that had already planted itself in all of us, the crops that were slowly growing into fields of heightened emotion and hate. I forgot the archive between my aunt and me, boxes of stories of betrayal and jealousy, that portended that Rima Mashi would (sooner or later) keep me at arm's length.

I looked at my Rima Mashi on those nights, so happy that someone was there to give me the sustenance my mother and Dida did not want to provide. While Rima Mashi may have always been a little distant, she was there for me, and it was all I could ask for. A person who remembered that I existed; who made me less lonely and ensured I was fed. I opened her tiffin carriers that overflowed with mangshor jhol, curry chicken, mustard fish and biriyani sprinkled with sliced almonds and golden raisins, and felt glee. Her food replaced the humidity of Kolkata with a honeyed and spicy aroma. My hunger—for company, for food, for recognition—was almost satiated.

Years later, Rima Mashi would tell my mother about how she looked after me when no one else wanted to.

My mother never thanked her.

14

EXACTLY A YEAR AFTER SHE abandoned me in India, my mother arrived for her first visit.

My mother was deeply preoccupied with how she presented herself to the world, particularly when she visited India to see our relatives. As ghosts increasingly nibbled at her mind, she began to dress less and less fashionably. Instead of saris threaded in gold, she wore plain salwar kameezes that hid the folds of fat that had developed on her belly. She stopped painting her lips maroon and red, and as she aged, her hair began to fall out. Her eyebrows were no longer thick and arched. She tried to hide the bald patches by etching her forehead with bobby pins. The rest of her hair she pulled back into a frizzy bun. I imagine stress, rage and her intermittent relationship with imaginary voices sent the long black strands twirling to the earth.

Rima Mashi and I picked her up from the airport. I was dressed in a long-sleeved burgundy shirt and jeans, a contrast to the clothes I wore at home in Pasadena that exposed my body and allowed the Southern Californian sunshine to tan my skin. As we waited for my mother at the airport, Rima Mashi firmly crossed her arms against her chest and vigorously chewed her paan. I noted the dirt under my Rima Mashi's thick, claw-like toenails. It seemed they had never been cleaned. I absorbed the contrast between my Rima Mashi and my mother, the fact that Rima Mashi now saw me regularly and my mother did not. I wondered if my mother thought about the state she'd left me in and the vast geographic distance between us; if she knew that even after she was gone, her voice remained a ghostly constant in my mind, fixed and audible in my psyche.

As I watched my mother walk towards us, I noticed that not only had her body and face changed but her clothes had as well. She was wearing a beige salwar kameez. Creases sketched across its surface, announcing how far it had travelled and how much time it had spent in airline seats and uncomfortable chairs scattered across terminals where she waited in transit—LAX, Tokyo, Singapore. Her kajol was smeared under her eyes and exposed the tiny lines that were slowly growing around them. The mother of my childhood would have washed her face and reapplied her make-up, changed her clothes and revealed herself to be fresh and buoyant. Nevertheless, there was still a youthful glow to her appearance, her cheeks flushed with hints of rose, her lips plump. And even though her hair was thinning, what remained was glossy and black.

As my mother reached for me, her body was stiff. Mine was as well. I could feel my soft skin turn angular and hard. I wanted two smooth surfaces to fuse into each other; the gentle force of a mother's touch. I wanted to love her without ambivalence, take in her presence without anger, but what came was the slow creep of rage that eclipsed the desire for the love between a mother and a daughter. Although I didn't want to see my mother or be near her, I resented her for being so far away. I believed that she had abandoned me, and now that she'd reappeared, she had no right to the title of mother she was attempting to reclaim.

We walked to the baggage carousel to gather her large suitcases. I silently picked one up, but my arms felt weak and clumsy. I wondered what American goods she might have brought with her. All around us, tired passengers hoisted their heavy luggage, the weight of each suitcase slamming into the floor—the clunky, sluggish sounds of arrival. Rima Mashi stood by the side, watching.

When we made it outside, the humidity and dirt of Kolkata embraced us. We found a taxi quickly. Rima Mashi sat in the front seat while my mother and I took the back. The road leading away from the airport was bumpy, and my head jostled left and right, right and left, as I absorbed the car's staccato rhythm. Gazing blankly out the window, I imagined my Dida lying on her bed at home, uninterested, her hands clasped in prayer, her head firmly placed on top of them. Would she even care that my mother had arrived?

The air in the backseat of the cab was stale, and my mother and I continued to feel awkward with each other. It was like we no longer knew how to occupy the same space. Our hands rested on the torn vinyl mere inches from each other, but we did not touch. Perspiration formed around our fingertips, leaving a wet imprint behind. Sweat dripped down my back. While I had begun dressing more conservatively in India, I'd worn extra layers that day, perhaps to perform my new modesty and reform for my mother. On some level, I wanted her to know that I'd changed. Despite my complicated feelings toward her, I still wanted her to be proud of me. I hoped we could get through the rest of her visit in peace, even as I knew peace would be impossible.

When we arrived at my Dida's flat, my Rima Mashi made us cha and jhal-muri. I savoured the warm, buttery potatoes, the slick texture of coriander, the mushy tomatoes and crunchy sev. We smacked our lips. Our teeth punctured crunchy peanuts to fill the void left behind by the lack of conversation. Suddenly, Rima Mashi spoke.

'Your hair is thinning there, no?' She forcefully pointed at the left side of my mother's scalp.

My Dida and Mashis had always called my mother 'chonchola', a Bengali term that doesn't translate well into English. The closest description is a person who is sharp, energetic and unstable, what in English might be described as a kind of mania. It was an apt description of my mother whose mind buzzed, like an electrical wire, with anxiety. Rima Mashi always knew how to tug the cord.

My mother's lips began to tremble. She stared at Rima Mashi, whose finger was exposing the flaw my mother had so desperately tried to hide. My mother touched the black bobby pins to make sure that they were still there, fingers moving shakily across metal and mane.

'No,' she said. 'I don't know what you are talking about.'

Water began to form around the ridges of my mother's eyelids. For an instant, I saw my mother morph into my Tapati Mashi. Her eyes seemed to fall inward. Just for a second, she had left us, her mind floating elsewhere.

I sensed an involuntary emotion, one I had felt long ago. I moved away from indifference and felt sympathy. I had a strong desire to shield my mother from Rima Mashi's examination and the force of her pointing finger. I was angry that she had named what everyone thought my mother couldn't be—plain—which my mother was not and would never really be. But she was a far cry from the beauty she had been as a girl and a young woman, and that was enough to make my mother feel inadequate.

Rima Mashi perhaps knew this. I didn't fully understand the encounter, but I sensed the resentments seeded there—a history of my Dida, who preferred her prettiest daughter and made sure the others knew that my mother was worth more than any of them.

The anger I felt towards Rima Mashi made my heartbeat hard and my breath hot. I wanted to soothe my mother and the demons living in her mind. I was alarmed by my reaction to Rima Mashi's statement and how it was beyond my own control. I wanted to hold on to the hate I felt for my mother. I wanted to revel and find joy in my mother's pain.

Instead, I felt love. It was so surprising.

I raised a cup of cha to my mouth and took a sip, swirling around the acrid taste of the black tea leaves, the watered-down milk, the spoonful of sugar. I chugged the feelings of love and protectiveness and swallowed them away.

During my mother's few weeks in Kolkata, I attempted to remain as obedient as I could under her fiery gaze—confine myself, curb my desires. We slept in the same room, each of us on the edge of our respective sides, careful not to touch each other.

But I couldn't change who I was. I wanted to hang out with friends and not her. My mother and I fought as we always did. I yelled at her; she grabbed my hair and pulled. Neighbours heard our cries, my mother's accusations, the insults that stung for days. When we fought, my Dida remained in her bedroom; there was no reason for her to intervene because conflict was a plush blanket of normalcy. My mother and I had inherited the violence between Dida and her daughter; my Dida must have felt comfort in the consistency.

When my mother left, I felt unshackled. I regained my freedom. And I turned towards my greatest desire in the world—finding a boy to love me.

15

A FEW MONTHS AFTER MY mother left, I found my first boyfriend. Aarush was in the year above me. I was fourteen. When I first joined CIS, I was struck by his jet-black hair and pale skin, both of which reminded me of Eric. He twinkled in the sun and captivated my attention. I stuttered in his presence. He was popular and knew the kind of hold he had on me.

One day, he decided to bring me to his spacious house. His floors were spotless, wealth articulated by clean and seamless furniture, no dust or dirt permanently packed into corners. Flamboyant artwork decorated his walls. His mother came home dressed in a gaudy salwar kameez, patterned with four-petal flowers.

'Aarush, why is there an Anglo-Indian in my home?' she asked.

I was startled. I didn't know what she meant. I didn't realize, at that moment, that I was little more than the make-up of my blood, a simple representation of a racial mixing that was unacceptable to many upper caste, full-blooded South Asians. But I could see a shadow of contrition cross Aarush's face; he was embarrassed that he had brought me into his home, that he had alerted his mother to his involvement with someone whose racial particularities she so clearly despised.

I had always felt shame over my identity. I did not embody the Indian ideal of fairness, like my mother. I tanned easily into a reddish golden-brown, and as I grew older and my skin darker, I was presumed by Americans to be everything but what I was—Native American, Mediterranean, Latinx, Middle Eastern, or just, *what are you?* Mine was also not the whiteness of Princess Diana, the woman my Dida adored, with her opaline skin and sunshine yellow hair. My skin did not shine as bright as pearls. My mixed race was clear for all to see—my half-whiteness, half-Indianness. The sight of me must have hurt.

In India, people stared at me on the street; I did not look like an Indian. When I approached vendors at food stands or in the open markets of Gariahat—amid the colourful spread of glass bangles in lime green and magenta, and the smell of fresh leather wafting from the chappals that hung from strings—and spoke to them in Bengali, they were always stunned that someone who looked nothing like them could talk in their mother tongue. I always responded by saying, '*Amar ma Bangali*'—my mother is Bengali. I was one of them.

Aarush's mother's tone, when she labelled me as an Anglo-Indian, affected me physically and involuntarily. I hung my head and hunched my back like my Dida. I felt an inability to speak. I later learned that Anglo-Indians were people of Indian and British descent, or people of British descent, born and raised on the Indian subcontinent. Some considered them remnants of the empire; they were kept at bay by bhadra society because they represented a time when lower castes could climb the ladder through racial mixing.[2] They weren't accepted by upper class Indians or by the British. They were neither here nor there. They lived in the interstitial space of the past and the future. Being half-white, I collapsed into the category of 'Anglo-Indian'. It didn't matter that my father had no English roots, that his family was made up of immigrants from Bohemia, Czechoslovakia. My mixed race must have been a reminder of a colonial legacy. The traces of this legacy were stitched over the entire patchwork of Bengali culture.

Aarush, while momentarily perturbed by his mother's observation, continued dating me. Late at night, on a train, during a school trip to Darjeeling, Mrs Iyer, our geography teacher—who hadn't been fond of me to begin with—discovered me in Aarush's sleeping cabin, our legs tangled up in the warmth of our fumbling teenage desires.

'Get up and go from here, Rani,' she ordered when she found us, our mouths attached.

I jumped out of Aarush's bed and ran to my compartment, where a few of my friends were slumbering, and crawled onto the slim, uncomfortable pallet. I fell asleep thinking about how Aarush's hard penis had pressed against my vagina. In my dream, I felt something acute rise up through my clitoris. It stretched towards a height that was nearly impossible to reach, found a peak and lingered there for just a moment, sharp and exhausting. I woke up.

In the back of my mind, I must have understood how much trouble I was in, but I pushed that knowledge away. Instead, I wandered about Darjeeling holding Aarush's hand.

'You realize these are the things that lead to being pregnant!' Mrs Iyer screamed at me later in the day. 'This is not how we behave in this country. It may happen in America ... but not here.'

Aarush was not present. He was not in trouble. He would be fine. He was a male from a wealthy family, and he would suffer no real consequences. He was one of the school's darlings.

In an unconscious effort to punish Mrs Iyer, I ate some Darjeeling street food on our bus ride down Tiger Hill. My body knew Kolkata's rastar-kabar. It had adapted to our local parasites. But food from the hillsides of Darjeeling carried bacteria foreign to me. I devoured momos with my classmates. Nausea took hold of me. I felt vomit rising, the curdled liquid teasing my throat. Instead of reaching over to Aarush, who was sitting beside me, his body up against the window, I walked down the aisle towards the front of the bus.

I'll ask the driver to stop, I thought. I'll throw up outside. I don't want to throw up on Aarush. If I can just get to the door.

Mrs Iyer was sitting in the front row near the aisle, her hair in her signature grey and black braid with its neatly stacked links. The end looked like the long stroke of an exclamation point. I tried to get to the door, but I couldn't hold on to that bile. It rose up and out of my mouth. It was an involuntary reflex, beyond my mind's control, beyond my ability to push it down by clenching my throat. As soon as I reached the place where Mrs Iyer was sitting, I vomited all over her head. Understandably, she turned toward me with a look of shock and disgust, the remnants of doughy dumplings dripping down her forehead. But her antipathy towards me had little to do with the fact that I had just regurgitated my meal all over her; she was repulsed by who I was—a bad girl—and my place in the school was now precarious.

When we returned from Darjeeling, Mrs Ganguly called me into her office. She looked at me with her caustic face, shreds of black-grey hair stuck to her cheeks. 'We will be calling your mother.'

I feared what the threat meant. I would be removed from school, and my mother would come and take me away, back to the United States in disgrace, to Mrs Clark's house. Or, perhaps, she would find a nunnery or Catholic missionary school, where they whipped and beat students into submission. Or, I would hear her say: 'None of them want you, a tainted girl, marked by the saliva of a boy!' I was not privy to the call between Mrs Ganguly and my mother. I only knew that my mother would be arriving soon.

After that trip to Darjeeling, Aarush broke up with me. He didn't want to be with a girl who was no longer attractive, who was becoming sullied, even if that sullying might have been, in part, because of him.

My mother arrived a few weeks after Mrs Ganguly's phone call.

'I don't want her,' my Dida yelled, pointing to me, finally articulating what I already knew.

My mother looked at me. She was confused. Who would take care of her daughter? She didn't know where she could store the fourteen-year-old body of a burgeoning girl, so that she would not bring shame to the family. I was a girl my mother was getting too tired—and too crazed—to handle. It was so late that no stainless steel pans clanged against each other, no propane gas seeped from the stoves that had cooked our neighbours' dinners. All that remained were the beeping cars of Kolkata, the insomniac sound of the metropolis.

My mother walked into my bedroom and pulled out a leather-bound book—my journal, pages and pages where I had scribbled *I hate myself* and *I love Aarush* over and over, the letters I'd written with such force that the pages underneath bore the indentation.

I had hidden the journal underneath my mattress. This was not the first time my mother had searched my belongings. Only her possessions had the right to remain private, like the photos of her indiscretions that she kept hidden in a shoebox in the farthest corners of her closet in Pasadena. She had always hated it when I had searched through her things without asking. It provoked the most remarkable fury.

She opened my journal and pointed at a page. She yelled so loudly I was sure she would wake our neighbours.

'What is this? What is wrong with you!' She jabbed at lines of *I hate myself*, and *I love Aarush*. 'Do you think a boy will give you more than I do?'

The journal fell from her hands, its pages tented on the floor. The sheaf of papers folded. My mother reached out for my ear and violently pulled it downwards. Then she pushed me, and I landed on the floor. My right funny bone hit the ground with precision, my eyes clenched from the electric pain that rocketed to my fingertips. I didn't fight back. It all happened too quickly.

Looking back, I think I intentionally left my journal in a place that would be easy to find. I'd wanted my mother to see my pain. I'd wanted her to help ease my body, my heart, even when I knew that was impossible. I'd wanted her to tell me that love was unfair—that the ones you love won't necessarily love you back.

I said nothing, gripping my injured ear. Finally, I removed my shoes and climbed into bed. In a foetal position, I closed my eyes and blocked out the wall in front of me. I heard my mother turn off the lights and put on the fan. I briefly opened my eyes and looked up to see the blades travelling round and round, cobwebs splattered across them. My mother laid herself on the other side of the bed. I could feel her gaze fixed on the opposite wall.

'I will deal with you tomorrow,' she said as she closed her eyes.

Neither of us could sleep. My mother began to whimper, 'No, no, no, no, no.' The rustle of her head against the pillow mimicked her language, expressed the desire for whatever-was-in-her to stop. I did not reach over to comfort her because, at that moment, nothing in my mind or body knew how. I thought

I was the reason for these ghostly beings and for a moment forgot that they had existed long before I had grown into a difficult child. I was not like my classmates. I felt the powerful forces of rebellion and desire stir within me.

During the time she was in Kolkata, my mother asked a few classmates' parents and grandparents if they would take care of me. She searched for a place where I could fit in. She approached a family of some schoolmates—a mother of two children I went to school with. Christopher and Nina were ten and eleven. Mixed race just like me. Their sister, Ela—a stunning girl with a symmetrical face, violet eyes, ivory skin, thick luscious brown hair—lived in Oslo with her white father. I was jealous of her. I wanted to be her. I wanted to touch her smooth ivory skin, unblemished and silky. Christopher and Nina's skins exposed their race—the white blood that ran through them—even more than mine. Their skin and eyes were lighter—Nina's a grey-blue that made her face burst with light. You could not see the melanin lurking under their skin like mine, melanin begging the sun to grace it so it could move to the surface. Their elbows and knees did not get ashy. Mine did.

As a child, my Dida would rub her elbows and knees with lemon, trying to annihilate the ash, claiming the acid would make it disintegrate. She would turn to me and point at the ash that had developed on my skin and cut another lemon in half. She'd grab my arm and the rub lemons vigorously upon my knees and elbows. She thought the acidic juices would make me as bright and white as the whitest of skin, skin that did not get ashy, that did not grow brown from the sun. It was a disappointment to her that somehow my skin had grown to be much more like hers than my mother's or father's.

I was sure that by living with Christopher and Nina, I would find meaning—meaning about myself, who I was, who I wanted to be, who I might become. They were disliked by the teachers at school, too—labelled as 'naughty' and 'unruly'. But they had powerful relatives. Their uncle owned two major newspapers in the region, each of which were our daily sources of news.

Christopher and Nina lived in a chic flat in a wealthy area. My mother and I walked into a bright living room; the sun's rays and the resulting shadows created a myriad of shapes across the walls. A Biedermeier sofa faced us; there was a quaint balcony behind it. A deep blue and red Persian rug ran across the floor of the room. In a corner was a small table with an elegant rotary phone—their own landline.

Two elegant armchairs. I sat in one, my mother in the other.

Christopher and Nina's mother's hair was fashioned in a stylish bob. Her skin was milky and smooth like her children's. My mother's skin was similar, but her hair was a bit longer, not bobbed or thick and stylish. Those familiar bobby pins lined the sides to cover her bald spots. Christopher and Nina's mother was dressed in black pants and a black shirt. My mother was dressed in a modest cotton sari. She looked awkward, like she was clumsily navigating her way through motherhood.

My mother told Christopher and Nina's mother about my bad behaviour, my sexual urges, how they were abnormal. 'I don't believe in premarital sex,' my mother said.

'I don't think it's good to stifle a child's sexuality, and I certainly don't believe that any of my children have to wait until marriage,' she replied.

I felt calmness overtake my body. This woman believed my sexual energy was normal.

'I think you're wrong,' my mother answered, as she scanned the sophisticated surroundings, the flat, so clean.

This was an age-old conversation—one ideologically charged, filled with opinions determined by religion, tradition, modernization, liberalism, and hopefully, most of all, care. My mother expressed her concerns, the thrust of her beliefs, which were slowly creeping towards religion and a deep preoccupation with traditional Bengali culture and the rules guiding a 'good family'. But her declarations lay in opposition to the life she had led—to her leaving India, when she was nineteen, to live in London, using the funds of a married man she had had an affair with; to her falling in love with a man who would abandon her; to her travelling to California to marry a white man twice her age. My behaviour, her hope was, would make up for her transgressions. Her reputation of being a good mother who raised a good daughter would overshadow her past.

'That is not how we behave in this country,' my mother continued, asserting the norms of Bengali culture.

'But you live in America, don't you? Things are different there.'

My mother expected a traditional Bengali mother, whose beliefs mirrored hers. This assumption was based on race, ethnicity and a shared culture. Her hands gripped the side of the elegant armchair. She had made her decision. I would not be staying with Christopher and Nina's mother. She was too dangerous.

My Dida was the only option. My mother promised my Dida that she would retrieve me after my exams in one year. She offered her money in return. My Dida agreed. I don't know why the school allowed me to stay for another year, but they did.

After my mother left, I began to develop cystic acne. My hands searched my face each night, travelling over the bumps that hurt so badly. Dime-sized lumps of pain forced me to realize the corporeal reality of my existence—an existence that evoked such a venomous response from family, friends, strangers, teachers, men. Some demon in my dermis was trying to crawl out of my miniscule pores, a demon that made my face hyper-visible, a face that wasn't nearly as beautiful as my mother's.

When I walked around my Dida's neighbourhood, my Rima Mashi and I would often run into someone who had known my mother and aunts when they were young and fresh, when bitterness and madness hadn't followed them like the dirty train of a gown that had been worn to one too many galas. The knowledge that my mother's half-white daughter had been forced to live in Kolkata because she was disobedient governed their gossipy whispers; rumours slithered through our neighbourhood.

'*Eta ke? Shukla'r meye?*' they asked.

'Yes, this is Rani, Shukla's daughter,' Rima Mashi would say.

'Pity,' the person would reply. 'She is not nearly as beautiful as her mother.'

I pined to be as beautiful as my mother. I felt my cysts bubble and grow in response to the fact that I was not. My fingers squeezed, rubbed, scratched and picked, as I tried to gain some sort of release. I created marks and crusty scabs all over my face, punctures to my skin that later formed shallow craters.

The history of my mother's beauty had taught me that beauty was the most important thing in the world. And here I was mutilating the only thing I thought I had to offer up—a pretty face.

16

DURING THE FEW MONTHS AFTER my mother's departure, I befriended a blonde girl whose family had moved to Kolkata from Tasmania. They were missionaries of some sort. She told me about god. No idols allowed, just one invisible god. I listened intently. I followed her lead. I attended her family's church, Assembly of God, in the hope that I might find answers like the ones my mother had begged for during our visits to Sai Baba or the nights she'd spent practising numerology. I absorbed the idea that false idols were evil. My Dida allowed us to have Bible study in her flat. She didn't care that these meetings condemned her existence. Maybe, if she had been invested in my life, she'd have liked my turn towards the Bible—any book would have been good enough, anything other than a boy. I looked good under the light of religious belief. But I never felt the heat of religious fervour; my body would not submit completely to an invisible god. Instead, I used him with purpose—the purpose of *looking* reformed.

Deepak was our Bible study leader. I was fourteen. He was twenty-two. I believed that his interest in me was indicative of his religious spirit, a spirit that demanded 'saving' people. I researched the idol-less god who he told me was *the* god. Knowledge had become a prescription for my achy soul. Deepak saw my sorrow. He felt my grief. He was older, wiser, a believer in something beyond Earth, and he seemed to look into the vast space of the universe for answers, where I imagined an imageless god might live.

'You seem to be in some kind of mourning,' he said, one day, as he lingered in my Dida's flat after Bible study.

'I don't know what it is. Or I don't have a name for it.'

'You are just looking for someone to love you, yes?' Deepak said, which at the time sounded profound, an educated assessment of my suffering. He had identified my condition—a broken heart. A heart broken by a mother. By a grandmother. By an irrelevant boy. It always helps to give suffering a name.

'Um, I guess? This boy. He broke up with me.'

'Well, I see a loving, kind soul in you. This boy doesn't deserve you if he can't see that.'

I began to admire Deepak, trust him, see him as an advisor, and, in turn, his interest in me grew. My wide eyes, filled with respect, must have been alluring. My sadness, provocative. I felt a slight shift in his demeanour. He gazed at me too much. He lingered around after Bible study too long. His body began to inch closer to me when we closed our eyes and held hands to sing to an elusive being. I felt his palms search mine for pleasure. My palms grew itchy from his touch, my body's way of warning me that his attentions were not innocent.

After four or five months, my mother arrived for another visit. I was on probation, and she had to make sure I was abiding by the rules—studying for my O-levels, not going out late at night, not seeking sustenance from a boy. Something had shifted financially as well. She now had enough money to visit more than once a year. There was a calm about her as she heard about the nights of Bible study, my trips to church, my conferences with the Bible study leader, Deepak. She knew something was coming, even if I did not.

His proposal emerged on the stairwell of my Dida's building. He was sitting on the stairs. My mother and I were standing.

'I will marry her,' Deepak stated, as he addressed my mother with confidence. He was leaking hope. 'I am in love with her. I can look after her, if you give me the chance. We can marry in the eyes of our god. I am gainfully employed. I will make a good husband.'

My throat stiffened and a deep nausea rose in my chest. I felt I might spit the bile that was rising into my mouth, reject him with the most wretched of bodily fluids.

'This might be the best chance you have, Rani,' my mother mused as she considered his offer. Her eyes began to blink.

I knew then that she might agree to Deepak's proposal, hand me over, leave me with a man she barely knew, a man whom I did not even want to be near. Wordless dread choked me as she dangled her control over my life in front of me. My body submitted to the terror with the same helplessness that I had felt the day my mother told me I was going to live in India and that she didn't know for how long.

'Please, Ma, please don't do this. I don't love him. I don't want to be with him,' I said, with shrill notes of desperation.

I grabbed her arm. My nails pierced her smooth skin. I wasn't trying to hurt her. I was trying to illustrate my despair. My pleading, begging self.

I now understand that, for her, this offer was not unusual. My Dida had been married at twelve. My mother had held on to my father (a man who was twenty-five years older than her) as an escape into a safe existence. Marriage would protect all of us. This was all she could ask for in my life. If I failed to succeed at school, to contain my desire for boys, why not give me to a man who wanted to take care of me and fuck me in the 'purest' of ways, with the blessings of a higher being?

I began to sob. 'I am fourteen! I am too young to be married!'

'It would be fine in the eyes of the church,' Deepak lied. 'We can wait until she is eighteen to be properly married. In the meantime, I will pay for her schooling and make sure she finishes her O- and A-levels.'

Gravity prevailed. I collapsed onto the floor, a sack of tears and pain.

'I will consider this,' my mother said. She looked directly into Deepak's eyes to see if he really was virtuous. She turned to look at me and I saw in her a possibility blossoming: escape. If she handed me over to Deepak, my mother would liberate herself from me. Was this the same relief I would feel twenty years later, when Rima Mashi would tell me that my mother was okay and that she would take care of her, each time I called?

I wondered: Did my mother really think she could find serenity if she gave me up? Could she not see that this was only the stillness before the tornado, because even if she wanted to, she could never get rid of me, at least in her mind?

Deep down, I knew this.

I looked away, as if this would relieve her of the burden of my appearance. She left Deepak and me to sort things out. I was still on the floor, Deepak on the stairs. Deepak's right hand lay on top of the Bible's black corrugated surface. 'THE BIBLE' was embossed in a large, bold font in capitalized letters, with 'Standard Written English' penned below its title.

Deepak must have seen himself as a holy person, there to rescue a young woman from a life of whoredom, to protect her from a tumble into hell. Inside, he was like most men, lusting after a fourteen-year-old girl's virgin body. But there was a book that proved his chastity and innocence. At that moment, I knew that I would never turn to religion again.

He put his hand on my shoulder. It felt like burning metal was branding my skin.

I lifted my head and looked at him. 'Do not touch me. I will never love you. I will never, ever love you.'

'I think in time you will. You will learn how deep my love is for you. You could love me back,' he said, gently, as if his soft tone would ameliorate my feeling of hatred.

I removed his hand from my shoulder as if it were a fly. I stood slowly. My joints ached from the time I had spent kneeling on the floor. I had always known that I needed to do well in school, needed to be a 'good girl' and prove myself. I had sensed that education could be my escape.

I now saw it clearly. If I chose to explore the force of my sexual interests, my mother would give me to Deepak, to save the family name, to prevent herself from being seen as a bad mother with a rebellious child. But if I chose education, if I washed away all fleshy desire, let it drip off me, I would be safe.

I walked into my Dida's flat, leaving Deepak behind. Cautiously, I approached the desk in my bedroom, where I had shoved the books that had bored me. I pulled out my macroeconomics textbook and looked at it, trying to kindle interest in gross domestic output, investments and capital. I sat on my chair and opened to that week's assignment—each paragraph blurred by my tears. I rubbed my eyes to remove the fog and began to read.

I developed a kind of determined studiousness, approaching my books the way I had approached Aarush's body. I put away my copy of the Bible and replaced it with textbooks for biology, mathematics and history, with plays by Shakespeare, novels by Jane Austen, essays by George Orwell. I learned to love *Pride and Prejudice*. I thought about the choices Elizabeth

Bennet had faced in the early 1800s. I considered her fight to defy the oppressive forces of marriage and the demands for women to conform to normative roles. I liked how strong she was. I had always read for pleasure, devouring trashy gothic romance novels, the short stories of Somerset Maugham and Guy de Maupassant. Why not read the literature I was assigned in class, even if Mrs Dutta glared at me over each and every interaction we had?

My mother did not allow Deepak to marry me. When she saw me sitting at my desk, a clothesline with kurtas and white saris behind me as I traced the lines of my economics book with a pencil and tried to decipher the meaning of each sentence, she believed that I had created a scene to temper her soul. I was on my way to being saved. I did not need the Bible; other books were enough to free me. My mother bought a ticket back to the United State and said, 'I will be back after you finish your exams.'

WINTER 2015
WOUNDED

WE FINALLY REACH THE HOSPITAL. The ambulance workers hastily transfer my mother to a gurney. We rush into an elevator and travel up three floors at a pace that feels infinitely slow, the second hand on a clock furiously trying to move forward in time. But I do not want time to pass. I do not want to lose this connection with my mother—her eyes on my face, my hands linked with hers, the warmth of her body commingling with mine. I don't want to know what will come next.

We enter a small room. The floors are dusty. A small window lets in some sun. Two nurses arrive and speak to me and my mother in Bengali. They call her Dida, and me Mashi, propelling me into an understanding that my mother and I have grown old. Somehow, I imagined that I'd always be my younger self; that my mother wouldn't age. She: forever Mashi; me: forever Didi. But I look at my mother and see that she is no longer Mashi. She *is* Dida. Which can only mean that I too need an older, different honorific.

I can see my mother's scalp, the beads of sweat that sit there among the thin silver and gold strands of hair. Her face is still youthful. Not many wrinkles define her eyes. There are no lines around her mouth. Her hair, her fragility, are what make her seem so old.

Maybe the nurses also see me as older than I am because they believe that somewhere out there, in the vast world beyond Kolkata, I am a mother. In that imaginary world, I have a baby girl. Maybe she looks more like Will than like me. Maybe she has blonde hair and blue eyes. Maybe she has skin as white as daisies. Maybe I have to slather vats of sunscreen onto my little girl's sensitive skin, something I never have to do for myself because I never burn. Of course, in the real world, I have no children. My mother is not a 'Dida'. And I am childless, because I want to be. I want to end the generations of mother–daughter strife.

The nurses try to remove my mother's jewellery—a diamond ring, a gift from my biological father, and a sapphire ring that an astrologer told her to wear because it would keep her healthy. The nurses lather my mother's hands with lotion, but the jewellery has not been removed for the two years she has lived with my Rima Mashi. Her skin is calloused around the edges of the rings, and as the nurses try and pull them off, her skin resists. They have to scrape off my mother's skin to remove them, leaving lines of blood across her fingers. She does not wince with pain, but I do. I want to absorb her pain and release her from the agony.

The nurses begin to undress her. They remove the blue and white nightgown and the pink sweater. When they gently ease her onto her stomach, we see the hole that has replaced the flesh on her lower back, a wound bigger than a full-sized dinner plate, white with pus, massive tendrils of dead ebony skin curling away from the interiors of her small frame, running from the dying bone within her. I can see inside her body. I can see dying bone. I can see the eggs of flies in her flesh, percolating. She is no longer human. She looks like meat on a butcher line. I should feel sick; instead, shock consumes me as I register the horrors that can happen to a human body, even whilst living.

One of the nurses looks up at me and asks in Bengali, 'Who has been taking care of this woman?'

I look down at the floor, stare at a slim rectangle of light—I imagine it as a beam of sunshine. *How did I do this to her? How did I let this happen? How did I not realize she was dying? Why did I abandon her? I am a terrible daughter*. I pull up my shawl and wrap it around my shoulders. When I raise my head to acknowledge the nurse's question, everyone stares at me with accusation. Shame pummels me.

'I live in America,' I try explaining.

But living in the United States is no excuse.

I look back at that hole in my mother's back, and I want to touch the edges of rotting skin, reach inside and search the interior of her body. Maybe I can find answers to our history, our love and hate. Maybe I can understand the tug of her hand on my ear, her belief in astrologers and holy men. Maybe I can discover the tapestry of her soul, covered though it may be in the calligraphy of her madness. I want to feel her agony and soothe the wound with my fingertips. I want to experience the months she has spent staring at the ceiling, waiting to die. I envision my mother gazing up at the fan in her bedroom, the cobwebs along its edges, silk woven from the spinnerets of a spider's abdomen. I imagine her reliving our thirty-eight years, all the times when we were alone together and the times when we were apart.

To me, it makes no sense—that my mother's body is in this state. I think of the times I've called and asked, 'Is she okay?' and Rima Mashi's response, 'She is.' Perhaps my aunt wished to spare me the agony of knowing; maybe she couldn't keep up with the demands of looking out for another; perhaps her reasons are not for me to know, only conjecture. I want to banish all possible scenarios. They lead me to a place that is dark and menacing.

What I do know is this—that my mother's body has disintegrated till it has ceased being beautiful.

What I will come to learn is this—that the spectre of my Dida, who was so warped by history's lessons that they unconsciously determined how she loved and hated her children, haunts my mother's ravaged body. I stare at the gaping hole in her back as it becomes a living metaphor for all that I have tried to learn but have never understood.

17

A GIRL NAMED SUMANA JOINED our school.

When she walked up to me and introduced herself, I was reading *Animal Farm*, sitting under an awning outside, where students studied on wooden chairs with wooden desks—these were only moved inside during the monsoon season. I recall trying to understand how each pig was a historical figure, how the book was an allegory for the failed Russian Revolution. I wanted to know the real meaning of a revolution, what historical upheavals portended, why societies were discontented with their rulers and how political thinkers tried to devise new ideologies that would save a people—although nothing ever did. Texts at school were beginning to captivate me.

I was surprised by Sumana's casual yet confident demeanour and was happy that there was someone new at school who didn't know about my bad reputation. 'I'm Rani,' I said. 'You sound like you're from America. I am, too.'

'Yeah, we just moved here from Philadelphia. My younger sister is here.' She pointed at a little girl with long black hair and big brown eyes that were as alluring as my mother's.

Sumana was adorable—five feet tall, with a tiny waist, a heart-shaped butt and a crown of ringlets, cut like a bob, that swung to her chin. She was incredibly wealthy. Her grandfather had been an industrialist. They owned property all over the world—New York City, Philadelphia and across Asia. I had not known that Indians could be so wealthy, with elevators in their houses, multiple cars and million-dollar paintings that hung from their walls. My limited childhood understanding of the world had made me assume that only white people could be affluent.

Sumana and I began to hang out all the time. I visited her mid-century mansion in Keyatala and her modern flat in Jodhpur Park, which had a winding staircase that led to her bedroom right smack in the middle of the floor plan. A large Swatch clock hung on her teal walls, and purple bean bags bubbled out from the wooden floor. I enjoyed riding in her chauffeured cars.

For some reason, her family didn't look at me the way the other parents did. Their eyes didn't turn into cat-like slits when I entered their homes. They didn't hiss about my ethnic make-up or my behaviour at school. They were too busy with their empire, leaving Sumana and me to play, and talk about the people, clothes and music we liked, as two teenage girls normally do.

We would travel to Peter Cat, our favourite restaurant, where we'd order the spiciest dish on the menu—chicken kalmi. One day, we were sitting on her bed, eating our take-out, while discussing beauty and boys. I told her that I felt ugly, that I was still heartbroken about Aarush, even though a few months had passed.

'He is mean. You are way better than him,' she said, matter-of-factly.

I was surprised. Aarush was socially accepted at school. Teachers crooned over him, while I was a pariah. How could I have been better than the boy who was loved?

'Really?' I responded.

Her nose was running from the heat of the green chillies that speckled the curried juices of the kambli. I picked up a piece of chicken. My mouth watered from the aroma of the thick broth, the knowledge that as soon as I took a bite, the spice would cut my tongue.

'Yeah, definitely,' Sumana said.

No one had ever reassured me in this way. No one had ever told me that I was too good for a boy whom I desperately wanted to love me. Sumana was the first person to ever articulate that sometimes the ones we love might not deserve our devotion. Sometimes they might even be cruel.

Ritwik was a boy who loved me.

He was in the grade above. Ritwik was an artist, a painter, a mad genius. He was swift with words, possessed an eccentric energy and was deep and insightful. He got the best grades in school and made people laugh uncontrollably with his wild ways.

He looked at me the way I looked at Aarush—with wistfulness. He always seemed preoccupied by my presence, as if I could give him what no other person in the universe could. He didn't seem to mind the marks on my face and claimed that he didn't notice their existence. But I did not reciprocate his feelings, and I don't know why. There is so much injustice in love. Loving someone does not mean they will love you back, and more often than not, we do not love the people who will treat us best. Ritwik knew I would never respond to his wants, and yet, he seemed to suggest that if he could be near me—my teenage body and mind—it could sustain him. Nothing felt perverse about his desires; his attention simply felt like devotion.

Ritwik drew me in with his intellectual musings, his art, his knowledge of books and music. We hung out, listening to Nirvana and Metallica in his room, his artwork all around us. I would pick up nude drawings of women he sketched in art classes outside of school and admire each stroke of charcoal, wishing I possessed his creativity, the ability to capture a moment or object, and gracefully reproduce what I saw on paper.

'You can have it,' he would say about so many of his pieces, and I gleefully took each one. Because of him, I developed a taste for the artistic, climbing the ladder from low to high art and literature, from V.C. Andrews to William Burroughs. I learned about Francis Bacon and Gerhard Richter. I hung each piece of Ritwik 's work on my wall, so that when I woke up in the morning, his sketches and paintings were the first thing I saw, distracting me from a stifling home and familial life.

My Dida didn't mind (or notice) that I spent time with Ritwik, and definitely not with Sumana. Her wealth made her the most desirable of all my friends. My studiousness was also enough to show the world that none of these relationships with boys was dangerous. I sat at my desk each night, pencil in hand, reading and rereading books I needed to master to do well in my O-levels. I never reached home too late, and Sumana and Ritwik came over often. By then, my Dida's depression had fully enveloped her, and she rarely got up from her bed. But Ritwik was the one person who could always engage her.

He'd tiptoe into her room and settle at the edge of her bed.

'Dida, *kemon acho*?' he'd ask. How are you?

Then, he'd get up and wiggle his body, swaying his hips from left to right as he raised his arms above his head, swirling himself around like an elongated inflatable man, to try to make her laugh. She did.

My Dida would not leave her flat for fifteen years. She wouldn't go to weddings or funerals or mukhe-bhaats. Her depression immobilized her, froze her in place, and trapped her in a space where traces of violence lived on every surface and ghosts of the dead floated around her. How odd that Ritwik was the last person on Earth to ever make my Dida smile.

Ritwik's family, as a whole, was artistic. His stepfather played classical violin. His family collected art from local villages to support indigenous artist communities. His mother, Kabita, dressed in silver and terracotta jewellery and earth-coloured saris with kantha stitching. There was nothing gaudy about her. In many ways, she was the exact opposite of my mother. Later in life, she would take over the role of my mother and help me.

Ritwik's biological father was different—more like my mother. He was filled with rage. One day, he was yelling at the barking dog that lived upstairs because it had been distracting him from his work. When Ritwik's father stopped yelling, he suddenly fell over. His head hit the wall. A streak of blood followed his body as it crumpled to the floor.

When I reached Ritwik's house that day, I found that a crowd of people had come to pay their respects. His father was draped in garlands of white rajnigandha. The room smelled sweet from the aroma of those flowers. I stared at the cadaver, the frozen face, the body no longer filled with thoughts, ideas or emotions.

I had been present somewhere in the room when my father died, but I was only two years old at the time; I could no longer recall his dead body. The only other dead bodies I had seen were the ones that passed by me on their way to the crematorium in Kolkata, corpses carried on wooden stretchers by men chanting, '*Bolo Hori, Hori Bol.*' I wondered why I didn't remember my own father's dead body. I somehow remembered other small things about him—how he defecated into a small bucket while my Dida took care of him, or how he carried me on his shoulders when he was still healthy—but I did not remember his corpse. Maybe I couldn't register the impossibility of the moment where my life had broken in half, when my mother and I had been left alone.

Ritwik was calm, as if his father's death had given him peace of mind. On that day, I saw no tears and no discernible sadness. A few months later, we were driving back from the Tollygunge Club—a remnant of the British Empire, where tea was poured from sterling silver jugs, and men in white uniforms made fancy cocktails for powerful, wealthy men. When we approached my Dida's building, Ritwik wailed. He dug his fingers into my forearm so I could feel his pain. His face pressed against my collarbone. I felt his tears drip onto my shirt; they soaked through to my skin. I put my arm around Ritwik's grieving body, thought of my own dead father, and grieved with him.

I finished my exams and received good grades, thereby proving Mrs Dutta and Mrs Ganguly wrong—I would not be a cautionary tale. When my results came in through the British consulate, Mrs Dutta reacted with surprise and self-assurance.

'It's always the ones we worry about that we discipline to do their best.'

Maybe she thought I would fall on my knees and shed tears of gratitude. Instead, I turned and walked away.

My mother returned shortly after, and she seemed something close to proud. I began to prepare for my departure, with a feeling of emptiness I could not have expected when I first arrived. I did not want to leave Sumana and Ritwik, my self-made family. My prepubescent desires had been flipped on their head in India. I no longer coveted the beauty of the white, blue-eyed, blonde girls in grade school. I wanted dark skin, brown eyes and the blackest hair. I wanted to drain the white blood out of me with a sieve. I wanted to look Indian.

The day before my departure, Ritwik and I were sitting on a short wall, Kolkata clamour all around us—feet stumbling along dusty roads, men with bullhorns campaigning for their political parties, blue-black crows loudly cawing. A little naked boy ran around us, his smile a bright row of teeth. He seemed happy, tickled by the world. His mother was by a kerb, periodically looking at her child, grinning at his playfulness, at his pudgy little legs and baby-smooth skin, at this being she had created, all hers, like no other creature in the world could ever be.

'We can adopt him,' Ritwik said.

'What?' I asked.

'We can adopt him and get married. That way you don't have to leave.'

It was a ludicrous idea, but Ritwik's proposal had been spoken in earnest, so unlike Deepak's desire to search my skin. I felt the pain in Ritwik's eyes, because he was losing me, because we would be 13,000 kilometres apart. We would never again live in the same city where we hung out every day and talked about music, art and literature.

I wore jeans and a burgundy V-neck the day I left, the same outfit I had worn when my mother had first visited that year after she had handed me off to my Dida. My hair was slicked back into a ponytail. A few photographs show just Sumana and me. I am embracing her from behind; her lips are pursed as if she is about to utter something. A slight smile crosses her face as she looks directly at the camera. Her body language is that of submission. We are kids—we have to submit to everything. In another photograph, my arm is wrapped around my head as my hand pulls back an errant strand of hair. Ritwik is there, too, looking at me with sadness, his melancholic gaze frozen in time. Unlike Ritwik I am smiling in the photo. But if there were a photograph of me moments later, sitting in the Singapore Airlines airbus, you'd see the tears tumbling down my face.

18

THERE WAS A QUIETNESS TO my arrival back in California. Something sleepy. I walked into my childhood home, lingering with each step, as I was flooded by a rush of memories that can only be described as nostalgic. Nostalgia re-envisions moments as unadulterated; the past is idealized as something different from what actually happened. And the longing for that more perfect version of events is visceral. You fall into the deep side of the sentimentality, recalling moments that never occurred—but how you wished they had.

I suddenly remember a small girl—three, four, five years old—who ran towards her mother with open arms, wearing a forest green dress that matched her mother's, a pattern of goldenrods across its surface. Sewn and designed by the one who had birthed her, the dress swayed left to right as she moved clumsily about, gesturing for an embrace. The soundtrack of Bollywood hits swam through the house and filled the little girl's ears with music. Her mother raised her arms, arched and dramatic, one bent above her head, the other stretched straight before her, fingers set in the style of an Indian dance—Bharatanatyam. She had been trying to teach her baby girl how to dance her favourite dance. The little girl looked up at her mother, who seemed so tall and statuesque. She knew there were moments when her mother stiffened with rage, when her mother held a wooden spoon she raised in the air, its destination the little girl's body. These were the moments when the daughter ran away—not towards; when she hid under her bed and in the sheltered corners of her closet. But in moments like this one, right now, she craved the softness and warmth of her mother's graceful body and shoved herself fiercely against her, gripping the torso with her small, plump hands.

A flutter of images travelled through the dark canvas of my eyelids each time I blinked. Reaching my room, I pushed open the white door to find the cobalt carpet faded but still thick and plush. The closet I had shut myself in so many times stood half-vacant to my left. To my right lay my twin bed with its brown duvet, in which my father had lain as he died. I sat on it, taking in the candied floral scent and recalling my mother's hair when I was little. Out of the window in front of me, I saw our tiny courtyard, fenced in by a steel gate with the letters SN and GN stamped onto it—Shukla Neutill, George Neutill. A gardenia bush was currently in bloom, the flowers bright white and waxy, the smell sweet and heady.

'Put your things away,' my mother said, jolting me out of my gardenia trance. She stood in the doorway, clearly wondering, like I was, how this was all going to work out. How would we live together? What would the next phase of life look like? How would time unravel? How would the two of us unravel?

'I don't have many things, Ma, but I will put them away.'

I got up and walked to my closet. Some clothes were draped clumsily on wire hangers. A few shirts—bright colours from the '80s—reminded me that a decade now had passed. I had no idea how I would dress, how I would move about the new-old landscape in which I had just landed.

I took one of the shirts off the rod and examined it. The rough cotton wasn't smooth and soft like the Indian kurtas and saris I was now used to. Suddenly, I craved that feeling of meticulously woven fabric. I tilted my head to sniff the air once more, unable to detect the lingering smell of mustard oil and garlic and ginger. I didn't know what my mother had eaten while I was gone, if she woke up in the middle of the night and made her rainbow snacks. I pictured her small body on one of our metal-backed kitchen chairs, a plate before her, a squiggly Bengali omelette on its ceramic surface, decorated with bright green chillies. In my imagination, her head hung down like my Dida's. Or like mine, when I felt defeated. She stared at her food, a Chinese numerology book on the octagonal table, her hand resting over its glossy cover. Did she think of me in those moments? Did she question her decision to leave me with my Dida? Did she long for the little girl who ran towards her? Was her bed cold at night, empty and desolate without my warmth?

Or did men join her, men whose names I would never know?

I looked away from this image towards the material existence of my mother. Still and silent, she watched from the doorway, her shoulder pressed against the whitewood frame. Her face seemed weary but alert. Her hair was unfurling around her face. She stood there, aware of my presence in her home.

'I will get everything in order,' I said, trying to reassure her that I would hang clothes neatly and make my bed each day, that I would not disrupt her space with my existence.

'Okay, good. We have a lot of things to do. I want you to rest and then say hello to the neighbours. It will be good to let them know you are home and pay your respects.'

One neighbour my mother wanted me to pay my respects to was dying.

'You must visit Mrs Gregory to say goodbye,' my mother instructed, eager to parade her newly reformed daughter, who was now mannerly enough to visit a sick neighbour and bring her the small bundles of Indian sweets and fruits my mother had sneaked through customs. My mother needed to prove that leaving me in Kolkata had been an act of good parenting. *Look at how well-behaved she's become. And she got straight As in her exams. She is smart, my Rani.*

When I entered Mrs Gregory's home, it smelled of old furniture, old appliances, old carpets, and an ageing body. She was lying in a hospital bed designed to keep her comfortable.

'The whole neighbourhood is disgusted by what your mother did to you,' Mrs Gregory whispered, her voice fading. 'Except for the Filipino family. I have no idea what they think.'

'What?' I asked, stunned. I vaguely registered that what Mrs Gregory had just said was racist, but above all, what I felt in that moment was defensive. While I still ached from the fresh pain of motherly abandonment—which would come to permeate my very being, shape every relationship I would ever have—I wanted, above all else, to spare my mother Mrs Gregory's searing critique

'How could a mother do that to her child?' Mrs Gregory continued. 'How could she just leave you there in India? It's terrible. And now, she's coming on to Peter. Trula told me, "That woman is out to take my husband. She is after his money." The poor woman, in her condition.'

Peter Reyes was our neighbour. He lived in the nicest house on our block with his wife, Trula. I knew him as Mr Reyes.

I could feel my ears turning red. Hot. I didn't doubt that what Mrs Gregory had told me was true. Yet, I felt absolutely repulsed by her accusation. I had the piercing urge to say, 'No! How dare you speak about my mother that way!' I looked at Mrs Gregory, an old white woman, dying, a catheter running down from beneath her thin blanket, her wrists frail, freckled, pale. Her veins shone blue. My head fell forward. I had no idea how to reconcile contradictory emotions.

'I hope you're feeling comfortable,' I said, ignoring her commentary on my mother's use of her femininity and sexuality to flirt with a married man, a man whom I had met when I was a child with no one to play with.

When I was younger, I liked to wander the canyon that surrounded our home. I would walk around all the manicured lawns, around the orange and lemon trees, sometimes falling to my knees in the dirt and grass, the skin rubbed raw and red, then pick myself up, dust off my knees, and continue to Mr Reyes's and Trula's home. They were childless. Trula would welcome me in to sit by her reclining chair, and I would tell her about my day. She'd give me small gifts—once, a small, smooth, orange sherbet marble jewellery box, where I'd put all the pennies I found.

Now, Trula was dying.

Mrs Gregory looked up at me. 'I am fine, just fine. How are you acclimating? Does it feel good to be back?'

I thought about how to answer this question without anger, without undoing my reformation. I wanted to hold onto the rare sympathy I felt. On the other side of the protectiveness I harboured for my mother was the desire to be seen as a child whose mother *did* abandon her, whose mother was indeed a bad and unruly parent.

'Yes, I am happy to be back,' I lied to her. Lying required no explanation of how I had grown to long for Kolkata's noise, dirt and dust. For the children playing on the streets with their bright, white smiles. For the friends who had come to love me. For the city itself, so alive, so unlike Mrs Gregory's old and dying body.

'Good,' she said. 'It must feel so very good to be back at home in sunny California.'

During my time away, my mother had become an entrepreneur. She had built a travel business, Answer Travel, and she ran it out of the study, from my father's large rectangular desk, which was heavy and dark and made of respectable mahogany. Her wooden-framed chair was cushioned with a soft, red velvet pad with sienna stripes. It was the chair my father had used while writing his dissertation on cancer patients and their dreams, a Jungian analysis of archetypes and death, disease and decay. He had finished his doctorate in psychology a few months before being diagnosed with cancer himself. His typewriter sat next to the table on a small shelf. It was black, with faded white keys; the skin of each one had turned beige from the sweat of my father's sticky fingers—perspiring from the heat and excitement of each sentence, each word, each letter, from the elation of translating interviews into paragraphs of argument and analysis. I envisioned my father, his long fingers gracefully typing away, only pausing when he misspelled a word and had to pick up the small bottle of Wite-Out to brush away the occasional mistake.

My mother marketed herself to the Indian communities that frequented LA County's Little India, Cerritos, printing flyers and posting ads in the local newspapers. She returned to her birth name; her business card now read 'Shukla Buku Bhattacharjee', not 'Sue Neutill'. This transformation, from the Americanized mother of my childhood back to the Indian girl she'd been before my birth, had occurred when I had not been there to witness the how and why. She must have wallowed in disappointment over the fact that her American dream of real estate investment was not to be trusted. As the 2008 housing crisis would later prove, American reliance on property was a farce—the promise of 'safe as houses' was a myth.

My mother formed a partnership with the local Indian wholesale sellers of tickets from Singapore Airlines. She cultivated these relationships. In return, she got free tickets to the locations where Singapore Airlines flew. This is how she travelled. This is how she saved our house.

She made a percentage off each ticket she sold. As I re-acclimated to the United States, our house was filled with the soundtrack of phones ringing throughout the day. While my mother was out, it was my responsibility to pick up the calls, saying, 'Answer Travel, how may I help you?' I would write messages down in the 'While You Were Away' notebook, filling out the names of the Indian customers who wanted to fly to Kerala, Mumbai, Delhi, Pune, Bengaluru or Kolkata. A huge map of Asia lay sprawled across a third of the mahogany desk, scratches all over it now from the force of her pen, her fingernails, her hurried writing. Her things were cluttered everywhere—her pens, her maps, her notebook. The desk looked less and less studious, less and less respectable, and yet ever more desperately seeking authority.

My tiny parade of reformation involved visiting our many neighbours, including Mr and Mrs Reyes.

'You're all grown up!' Mr Reyes exclaimed when he first laid eyes on me. 'You've become such a beautiful woman. You know, they say that Indian women are the most beautiful in the world!' He beamed, as if he wanted to be a part of my transformation, proud of a daughter and the woman she had become.

Trula was there, too. She was lying on her tan leather reclining chair next to a sliding glass door. The smoggy LA skyline, its blazing sunrises and pastel sunsets, were her view. She was sick, slowly dying from heart disease and old age. But she was happy to see me, even though my mother was trying to steal her husband, lure him away while she passed quietly through the final days of her life.

I knew Mr Reyes would become a lasting presence in my life. I could tell by the look on his face, that of a man who desperately wanted to be a father. I could also tell from the way that my mother strolled down our cul-de-sac, past his house, a smudge of lipstick defining her lush lips. When trash day came, I would notice her persistently look out the window. When she'd hear the scrape of a garbage can down the street, she would sneak outside to see who it was. If it was Mr Reyes, she would bring out our trash and gently place it on the curb, careful not to scare him away. Then, she would walk down the street to say her 'hello' and 'how are you' and inquire about Trula and her health. The real questions were always: 'When do you think she is going to die?' And: 'When do you think you will want me?'

She began to ask Mr Reyes for help, especially now that her daughter was back home and she was a single mother running her own business; she needed him to drive me here and there, pick up small things for her from the grocery store. There was no limit to the help she could ask for or the small talk with which she could engage him. And he obliged. He was happy to assist the only single mother who lived on his block.

Those first few weeks back, I walked alone through the canyon once again, hiking, expanding my radius beyond our immediate neighbourhood. I trudged up the steep hills to the edges of the San Gabriel mountains. I heard the leaves rustling with wildlife, smelled the aroma of pine and eucalyptus. I found a waterfall, thin and glorious; the sun beat down on its steady flow as it cascaded onto grey rock. I sat next to it. A slight spray of fresh water freckled my skin, the drops like tiny jellyfish swimming off my arms and legs. I closed my eyes and ached for India, the place that I now considered home.

Everything around me was so clean. Too clean. There was smog, yes. But it wasn't a dense wall of smoke forged from burning trash; it didn't sting your nose. This pollution, perhaps more insidious in Los Angeles, pretended not to be as bad as the smog in the 'developing' world. It was more sterile. Freeways sprawled past the suburb, a flatland interrupted by an immense mass of diamond-shaped mountains.

And the silence. In Pasadena, our home was couched in the edges of the wilderness. Deer, spotted rabbits, and even baby bears and their mamas roamed around us, but they never made a sound. So much quiet, almost frightening in its emptiness. I wanted noise. I wanted to feel the hard beat of a drumming city. I wanted cars beeping—so many cars beeping. I wanted proximity to thousands of people, to know that if I screamed, someone would hear me.

19

SOMETIME IN THE MIDDLE OF the spring semester, I entered Alverno High School, where I was thrown once more into an American curriculum. I was only fifteen, but I was placed in the junior class (normally the grade for someone who is seventeen), because of my rigorous Indian education. Suddenly, I was learning about the American Revolution and picking up Spanish, a language that somehow came naturally to me. I learned how to take multiple tests that slowly shaped my final grade. At Calcutta International School, our years were spent reading the same texts, preparing for a single final exam that we were expected to take at the British consulate. In some ways, O-levels were like the SATs—one exam that determined what you had learned. But the classes at Alverno felt different because many things shaped your grade—participation, essays, tests and effort. A grade wasn't a cumulative assessment of your knowledge. It wasn't a few hours of an exam that was supposed to be a definitive measure of a student's intelligence.

Literature had become my favourite subject, both at CIS and at Alverno. At Alverno, our English teacher, Miss Timony, exposed us to a wide range of texts. She was unlike any teacher I had ever had. She did not stare at me with disgust and disappointment the way Mrs Dutta had. Rumours hinted that Miss Timony was a lesbian. I had never encountered a person who was openly gay, whose desires veered away from what was considered respectable. The same desires resided in me, stowed away in my unconscious; I still carried the memories of watching *Purple Rain* and the feelings Apollonia's breasts provoked in me. But I didn't have the vocabulary to understand the attraction as a kid. I didn't even have the words with which to phrase my questions. No one at school discussed that desires were complex and didn't necessarily lead to marriage between a man and a woman, which was the story I'd always been taught. My sexuality was designed to consider both men and women as objects of lust.

Miss Timony was not afraid to talk about sexuality, race and class. Suddenly, I could name emotions, fears and confusions I had never been able to articulate. I was rivetted by discussions of race. In Kolkata, we did not read Jane Austen through the lens of colonialism—even if it always hovered in the shadows. Instead, we focused on linguistic style. We never questioned the imperialism that asserted itself in *Pride and Prejudice* or where Mr Darcy's family had got its wealth. We didn't even ponder over the role of feminism in the novel, or how marriage had been a means of survival for women, as it had been for my Dida and mother. I had noticed these omissions in the curriculum during my O-levels, but didn't possess the precise words to describe why discussing these issues mattered or how they translated into lived experiences. In Miss Timony's class, we openly addressed the politics of each text. We wrote papers about Sandra Cisneros's *The House on Mango Street*, Fannie Flagg's *Fried Green Tomatoes*, Maxine Hong Kingston's *The Woman Warrior* and Toni Morrison's *The Bluest Eye*. Suddenly, brown and Asian people came to life in the pages of books. Words like 'racism' gave me a vocabulary to understand moments from my childhood when the popular girls had complained about the smells in my house, when they'd mocked my mother's accent, when I, myself, had embraced the idea that blonde and blue-eyed girls were prettier than brown ones. The subjects of the novels Miss Timony assigned felt more familiar than the world of the lily-white British heiress, whose worst horror was needing to marry a commoner.

Amy Tan's *The Joy Luck Club* was my favourite. I would be trained to critique the novel later in life, when I became indoctrinated by literary criticism and educated by the elite; I would complain about its problematic representation of Asians and Asian Americans. But at the time the book came out—and the movie, too—I loved how it described immigration's impact on generations of mother–daughter relationships. *The Joy Luck Club* was something when I had nothing.

Our homework was to read the novel and watch the film. My mother and I went to see the movie together. We walked into the theatre, and I ran my fingers against the theatre seats, wondering how long the film was, how much time I would have to spend near the only guardian I had. When we sat down to watch, the darkness of the theatre enveloped us, as if night had suddenly fallen. The projector was the moon, and the highlighted bodies were the comets and stars. The story moved me in the most sentimental of ways. My hatred towards my mother began to drift away; we moved into a cinematic universe where we mirrored the women on screen. This was a parallel galaxy where the strife of our relationship was replaced by love and mutual understanding.

As I watched these Asian American women fight with their mothers, I understood how cultural cues and contexts could be misunderstood; that mothers could carry histories that their daughters couldn't even imagine. I wondered if my own mother had endured the horrors these women on the screen had suffered—they had migrated across oceans, they had survived abusive husbands or the Japanese invasion of China. Maybe this long history of violence against women was the root of the strife between my mother and me. Was that all that divided us—the conflict between immigrant parents and first-generation children? I wanted the explanation to be this simple. I cried.

My arm crept towards my mother's hand. I reached for it and held it. My fingers explored the smooth surface of her palm. She consented to my touch. She was gentle, tender in a way that had left her over the years as she became hardened by loss, by dissonance with a daughter whose force of will was as powerful as her own. Of course, the cause for our conflict didn't just lie in simple cultural misunderstandings. It was more nuanced, hiding in the grey areas of life and the complications of the history of our family—a grandmother who hated herself because she was brown, a mother who bore the weight of this hatred because she was light-skinned.

But that one day, in the womb of the theatre, under the movie's spell, I let go of my unwavering bitterness for a few hours. I searched my mother's hand for meaning.

While I had been gone, my mother had become completely averse to Western medicine. Maybe the voices and imaginary beings she lived with told her to reject it. Maybe the Western world was a place she felt she didn't fit in. But neither was the East—though, now, she was fighting her way back in.

She did yoga, but her body did not bend the way that tall, lanky, white ladies could, like oiled hinges, when they did Chaturanga Dandasana. She shopped at local health food stores for vitamins and herbs. At the time, none of her behaviour seemed irrational. Organic produce and supplements were in vogue. We were starting to learn about the evils of hormones in food, the pesticides sprayed on fields of budding vegetables, and the illnesses these poisons induced.

Slowly, my mother had moved away from the flavourful delights of Bengali cooking. No meat, and less and less fish, which had always been her favourite. I now understood why the aroma in our home had been flat when I returned. No tang of green chillies or bitter turmeric, the blinding burn of red onions flecked with chilli powder.

Earlier in life, my mother had craved savoury, spicy heat, a sting to her tongue that made her mouth froth with saliva. She dismissed the food white people ate. Her palate rejected bland, dry, boneless chicken breasts, Wonder Bread, pork chops and hamburgers. She cooked with ghee and ate Indian vegetables with no English names—lau'r torkari, for instance. Now, she began to forgo the food she loved in an effort to control both her bodily and mental health. Her newfound interest in Ayurvedic medicine led her to believe she had Pitta Dosha—fire energy—which meant that she needed to cut out items that fuelled heat in her body—green chillies, garlic, mangoes sprinkled with salt and chilli. She tried to dull her senses, so she could control her fury, eschewing all food that Ayurvedic doctors claimed might ignite her rage.

Sometimes, though, I caught her cheating.

One weekend, she took me to Cerritos and bought me some masala dosa. I pulled bits off its long cylindrical body and dipped the crusty pieces into sambhar and coconut chutney, as I had when I was a child. She didn't order anything for herself but watched me as if she had lost something and lustfully wanted it back. When I went to the bathroom to wash my hands, I returned to find the remains of my dosa gone. My mother tried to hide the evidence of how she had cheated, hastily licking away the dots of creamy coconut chutney at the corners of her mouth. She looked up at me and said, 'I can't help it.'

I understood.

20

EVEN AS MY MOTHER TRIED to quell her desires, she moved in on Mr Reyes.

Trula's health had rapidly declined until she had passed away. We went to her memorial, and my mother offered herself up as comfort and company. She let Mr Reyes know she was there if he needed her. A man who had been married for forty years was used to having someone near him, and my mother sensed this. She couldn't help but seduce him, just like she couldn't help but cheat with her food; her drives always defeated her desire to be subdued. She had been alone for more than three years in our house; she had been a widow for thirteen years; she must have felt palpable longings for another body in her bed.

The neighbourhood gossiped. 'He is twenty-five years older than she is. Look at her taking advantage of a grieving man!'

Mr Reyes had been born in the early 1920s in California, the son of Mexican American parents. 'People always ask me what I am,' Mr Reyes often told me. I admired him, his ability to respond to white people who asked about his racial identity. Like me, in diverse California, he was often mistaken for Native American or Filipino, but never for who he was.

'What do you tell them?' I asked, curious, though I didn't precisely know why.

'I tell them I am a Californian, that I'm an American!'

'What do they say?'

'They laugh.'

During our fights, I always had an impulse to push my mother—put my hands on her shoulders, sink my thumbs into her collarbone, and propel her to the end of the room. I imagined her head hitting the wall, blood emerging from her skull, her body crumpled up on the floor, stiff and lifeless. I imagined the police.

One fight was different.

It was afternoon. Mr Reyes was now a daily presence in our life. I always called him Mr Reyes as a term of affection because my mother never used his first name. She had given him his own dak-nam, a Bengali pet name, Señor Reyes, for she spoke Spanish fluently and they often spoke it together.

Mr Reyes's fatherly affection was confusing, and I had found myself suddenly craving memories of my biological father. I searched our home for the tapes of my father's voice, and found them, tucked away in the innermost corner of my mother's closet, with some jewellery—a pearl and ruby brooch, a few pendants and an old Rolex that had my father's initials engraved into its thick, silver skin. I placed the brooch inside my pocket, knowing it belonged to my paternal grandmother, a woman I had never met and from a family I had never known. My mother had slowly begun to remove my father's remnants from the house. Photos of him holding me as a newborn that had once lined the walls of our hallway and the space above the mustard couch in the living room were now gone. I had no idea where my mother had placed these images. I wandered over to the TV room to listen and remind myself that my father once existed. My mother found me with the box in my lap, the watch in my hands, my ear against the speaker, my father's voice in the air.

'What is this? You went through my things without asking? Why did you go through my things?' my mother asked, her voice climbing towards a crescendo.

'I just wanted to play the tapes,' I said. My fingers rubbed the thick glass of my father's watch, my eyes turned down, concentrating on the chestnut face and the silver dial.

She snatched it from me, furiously. 'This doesn't belong to you.'

'I know, Ma, I just wanted to see some of his things.' My voice trembled. I began to concentrate on not crying, knowing that the act had long infuriated her. I clenched my jaw and stiffened my throat, my teeth pressed into my tongue.

'I don't know why you're so interested in him. He didn't want you. Mr Reyes would have been a much better father. He is the one you should be interested in!'

Mr Reyes's presence *did* feel paternal; I knew he wanted a child, as much as I wanted a father. But my father had died when I was two years old. Having a father figure in the house felt wildly unfamiliar and I feared I might also be betraying my biological father by embracing him. If I let Mr Reyes occupy a space that my biological father had barely been in, would I suddenly forget that my father had actually existed? In so many ways, I already had.

Mr Reyes, of course, had always wanted a daughter—each time a baby girl passed his line of vision, a melancholic smile passed over his face. I knew that, at sixteen, I was older than the child he wanted, I already had been shaped by my mother, but Mr Reyes saw that I needed someone. That need pulled him towards me and my mother, perhaps even more than my mother's advances.

Mr Reyes was well-off. A landlord of multiple properties, he could give my mother what my Dida had wanted all her life—

money. My mother's beauty and her need for a father for her daughter were the perfect bait.

'Ma,' I yelled, 'he was still my dad.'

'I am telling you! He did not want you! I did! I had to pull out my diaphragm. You were *my* choice, not his!' she said, with spite.

Her statement assaulted me, punched me down in size. I knew that part of what she said was true.

My mother shook from the force of a thousand memories of treachery. She threw my father's watch across the room. It hit the metal handle of our sliding door, and the thick glass façade cracked and shattered all over the floor. The chestnut face was now naked, the moving hands exposed.

I set the box that held my father's voice onto the floor and slowly stood. I wanted to smack my mother, push her. But sadness prevailed. The tears were unstoppable. I walked to our front door. The only anger left inside me slammed it shut. I walked down the road to Mr Reyes's house and rang his doorbell. He only took a few seconds to open the door.

'Hi there. What is it, honey?' he asked, unable to ignore the tears running down my face.

'Can I stay here?' I asked.

'Of course, come on in. You want to lie down?'

I nodded as he led me to his guest room. I looked over to the white reclining chair next to the wide window; Trula used to lie there, staring out. Mr Reyes looked over, too. I could sense his sorrow, our mutual melancholy. He put his hand on my back; it felt warm. His touch was the melting grace of the sun. I walked into the guest room, so orderly, no piles of old underwear, no papers stacked up without organization. His house was clean and clutter-free, miles away from the fragmented space that my mother and I called home. A Japanese-style bed frame beckoned, along with a duvet cover of royal blue with white morning glories. I lay down and hugged my knees into my chest. I felt my grandmother's brooch in my pocket, its lumpy shape digging into my skin.

'I'm about to go out for a little bit, maybe a half hour, maybe less. You stay here and relax. You can have anything you like in the fridge. There is orange juice and milk, and if you're hungry, there is some cereal in the cupboard to the left of the sink.'

I shook my head and fell asleep.

When Mr Reyes returned, he was carrying a small paper bag. I opened my eyes for a moment, and he put his hand on my forehead to check my temperature.

'Go back to sleep. I just made you some keys to the house. You can come here whenever you need to, okay? You're always welcome in my home. Whenever your mom and you are fighting, just come here.'

And I did. So many times that year, I did.

When I finally returned home, my mother wasn't there. I searched her room for the tapes of my father's voice, making sure she wouldn't be able to find evidence of my foraging. But the box was nowhere to be found. I walked to my bedroom and placed the brooch inside a vintage suede boot, tucking it all the way in. My hands pushed it to the edge of the toe, as I feared the possibility that my mother might go hunting for it. I lay down on my own bed—my father's deathbed—and thought of Mr Reyes, his warm paternal touch, his walnut-coloured eyes filled with deep sadness as he mourned the woman who had recently left him. Somewhere in those eyes, there was also hope—hope from the two women who had entered his life.

When my mother came home, she carried bags from the local organic market, some food from their deli, tasteless vegetables and brown rice, hummus and edamame. We ate in silence.

A few weeks later, I would muster up the courage to ask her for those tapes.

'I don't want to go through your things, Ma. I was just wondering if I could have my father's tapes?'

'I threw them away.'

'What? When?'

'It doesn't matter. You don't need those tapes. Mr Reyes is going to be your father.'

Did she think the remnants of my father would drive Mr Reyes away? Did she want to move forward and never look back? I do not know.

I walked to my room to grab Mr Reyes's keys, stopping only to bury my hand in my brown suede boot to recover my grandmother's brooch. I stumbled my way to Mr Reyes's home and opened the door. He was inside reading *The Los Angeles Times*, snacking on pistachios.

'Hi, honey.' He saw the tears in my eyes again. 'You want to lie down again?'

'Yes, please, and can I leave this in the guest room?'

I opened my palm to show him the brooch.

'Of course you can. Just put it in one of the drawers.'

I kept that brooch there until I left for college, never once letting my mother know that I had stolen it. Mr Reyes didn't ask me where it came from, nor did he mention it to my mother. The brooch was our little secret.

It feels like a cliché to write about when I left for college, but the day I did, I felt the overwhelming power of leaving my mother.

I had got into a college all the way across the country. When I received my acceptance letter, I shrieked with joy. My mother rushed to the hallway where I stood; I was gripping the acceptance letter so tightly that I almost ripped it in half.

'What is happening?' she asked.

'I got into Boston College!'

My mother looked happy for about a millisecond. Pride. That was what I saw—a motherly sense of pride. And then that flicker gave way to the more familiar worry and anger.

'How are we going to afford this?'

'My counsellor told me there will be a financial aid package. We have to apply for loans.'

'We shall see,' she curtly replied.

Those months before I left for college, my mother constantly threatened not to pay my expenses, not to sign for the loans. I, in turn, threatened to apply to be emancipated. My feet were arched and ready to sprint away from her.

Mr Reyes intervened each time. He sat with me, and we applied for every grant we could find. When he offered to pay for my first year, as he and I sat at the kitchen table and looked through applications, my mother knew that he would be in her life for the rest of his days, and money wasn't going to be an issue ever again.

My mother and Mr Reyes married exactly six months later, when I was filed away in a new existence. I didn't register the financial security that came with their relationship. Despite a childhood filled with my mother's financial woes, I took the allowance Mr Reyes afforded me for granted. I could never fully comprehend the ways in which my mother's beauty provided me with privilege and wealth. My mother, on the other hand, no matter how rational she was about her newfound wealth, would fret over money for the rest of her life.

My mother and I fought so badly during the days leading up to my departure that she refused to travel with me to see the campus or even to say goodbye. Instead, Mr Reyes and I would fly together. He would be the new parent.

I had just turned seventeen years old. On the day I was to leave, Mr Reyes waited in the car.

My mother walked with me slowly to the large wooden front door.

I reached for her and felt her tense as my arms fell around her small frame.

'Bye, Ma.'

She didn't speak. Instead, she nuzzled her face into my neck, and I felt my shirt become damp with her tears. I collapsed into her and a temporary amnesia. Then, memories of all our strife came back like the thick rain that falls so heavily you cannot wipe it away. I gripped her shoulders and moved her away from me. When my mother finally looked up to confront my departure, her tears were gone, and her eyes looked like large, hard periods at the end of a sentence, glaring and definitive.

I mirrored her eyes and became a full stop, too.

What followed was the white space after the end of a chapter.

'Fine, then,' I declared, and she did, too, with those glassy periods for eyes.

As I left her, I remembered the day she left me in India. Now I was leaving her. And I felt free.

But I knew my freedom was an illusion. Would I ever really be free from my mother?

21

I WAS IN MY SECOND year at college when I asked my mother to go to family therapy.

I arrived at LAX to see her waiting at the gate; Mr Reyes was by her side—still the days before 9/11, when passengers could be greeted immediately upon arrival.

My mother stretched her arms to embrace me, and I wanted to welcome her touch. Instead, I stiffened. My skin turned inward, creeping away from her affection, even as I recalled the day she visited me in India for the first time since her departure. My mother felt my repulsion, and her body became concrete. As she looked me up and down, taking in my black motorcycle boots, tight black pants and leopard print shirt, I felt her disapproval and dismay. A small tattoo peeked out from under the sleeve of my shirt; she looked at it and said nothing.

She had been married to Mr Reyes for a year. They were living together in his home, and when I reached Mr Reyes's residence, I saw how my mother had imposed herself on his space. The house that Trula had built with fastidious attention to interior design was now in disarray. The mid-century furniture was mismatched, with my mother's '70s velvet sofa and armchair. Heaps of vitamins and herbs were strewn all over the house. She had thrown away Trula's long shelf of cookbooks and replaced them with texts on Ayurvedic medicine, yoga and meditation. She believed these would quiet her mind.

This was my first trip to LA since I had left for college. I refused to visit with greater frequency, and even now, when I was here, I could not bring myself to be near my mother for more than three days at a time. I was only in my late teens; still, I questioned why I was returning to the woman who drove me mad. I wondered what pull she had over me. A part of me yearned for my earliest years of euphoric love, the days when I had been in awe over her beauty, when I had been consumed by her body.

In the year I had been away from her, my mother had called me constantly. It was a strange reversal from the days when she wanted to be far away from me, leaving me with Mrs Clark and my Dida. Now, she wanted Mr Reyes to have the daughter he had always pined for. She wanted a nuclear family, maybe even a semblance of normalcy, even though she must have known that we would never achieve domestic tranquillity.

'Come with us to Shanghai, I will pay for it,' she'd say. 'Don't you want to see Mr Reyes? He is getting old.'

She'd detail a laundry list of gifts that she would give to me if I visited her, if I conveyed to her that I loved her, if I could stand to be near her for over three days.

But I was determined to be independent. I moved off campus in my sophomore year and rented a small room with barely enough space for a futon and a desk in an apartment a few miles away from school. I worked at Bread and Circus—twenty hours a week in the bakery department—so I could pay my rent. I told my mother nothing about my life.

Deep down, I wanted her to apologize for leaving me in India. For subjecting me to her madness.

But she never did.

Instead, she yearned to rewrite our story.

'I had to leave you in India!' she would yell. 'Look what it did. You are so good in your studies.'

I did not capitulate and say, 'You did the right thing. I am a good girl because of your actions.'

College became my psychic refuge. The chastity belt that had been wrapped around my genitals since my time in India fell off. As is true for so many, losing my virginity felt anticlimactic. My first sexual encounter was mechanical. I chose a boy I was barely attracted to and was more concerned that he put on a condom than that I experience any pleasure; I didn't want to become pregnant, and if I did, I knew I would rush off to get an abortion.

The intellectual curiosity that aroused me the day Deepak asked my mother if he could marry me was more important, I decided, than sex. I would rather be a brilliant academic than have an active, satisfying sex life. I didn't realize that I could have both.

I began my swim through the world of the humanities. I took classes in Women's Studies and English that introduced me to literature I had never encountered—Salman Rushdie, Amitav Ghosh, V.S. Naipaul, Hanif Kureishi, Sara Suleri, Jamaica Kincaid, Bessie Head and Chinua Achebe. I was introduced to psychoanalysis, and the intersection of the two fields—psychoanalysis and postcolonial literature—blew my mind and fuelled in me a desire to know more. Here, in these books, I would uncover answers to my family's behaviour.

I read Freud. In his writings, I found a sexist but provocative understanding of 'the mother'. I sat at a desk that a friend had given me, designed for a little girl, smoking cigarettes and drinking coffee and pondering over his theories about a girl's attachment to her mother, stronger and more powerful than a boy's. I questioned his view that a girl's detachment from her mother was essential if she was to desire her father and become a heterosexual woman. I thought about his description of the break between mother and daughter—how it could manifest itself in excessive hostility, sometimes bordering on violence. While the budding feminist in me thought that most of Freud's theories were problematic—and my Women's Studies professors nurtured this critique—and while I found nothing in his work that addressed madness or paternal absence, racial difference, cultural mores or colonialism, what rang true for me was his analysis of the attachment bond, the ambivalence and the hostility between mother and daughter.

Days of reading postcolonial novels, nights of unravelling Freud and Jacques Lacan, Julia Kristeva and Gayatri Spivak, made me realize that therapy could help me, help her, help us. So, on that first visit home, I decided to ask my mother if we could find a therapist to soothe our mental wounds and rekindle an uncomplicated, unambivalent, fierce attachment to her.

I walked into the guestroom and put some of my underwear away in the dresser but kept all my clothes in the suitcase in case I needed to escape. I pulled out a notebook; the paper felt dry against my fingertips, worn from doing dishes at my job at Bread and Circus, and the nights spent tapping at my computer keyboard, musing upon the meaning of psychic wounds and attachment. I wrote down the hours of each day I would be in California, and every time an hour passed, I decided I'd cross it out, counting down—a practice similar to the games of numerology my mother had played when I had been a young girl. I recalled how she would wake me in the middle of the night to sit in our hallway, a pair of dice in her hands, her long black hair dusting the sepia tiles. I discovered that I had inherited her reliance on numbers to get through time; it became my method of coping with my mother's presence. I also counted objects to determine good or bad luck. I don't know where I picked up the practice—I could not help but believe that seeing single objects meant bad luck and seeing things in pairs meant good luck. Every day, I searched the blue sky above me for two birds instead of one. I believed I would have a good day if I saw two waving their wings in unison. I could not shake off the feeling that certain objects were blessed and determined a safe and happy future. I was my mother's daughter, even if I vehemently wanted to deny that her convictions had infected mine.

I crossed out an hour in my notebook and walked into the living room, where my mother was watching a recent Bollywood blockbuster. Tablas played in the background as I broached the antidote to our strife.

'Ma, I think we should go to a therapist.'

Her response was immediate. 'There is nothing wrong with me!' she retorted defensively. 'You get this from your *father!* All this mental nonsense! Not from *me!*'

I was startled and frightened by her anger. My stomach punched with fear. I don't know why I was surprised by the immediacy and violence of her refusal, but I was.

I now understand that most likely my Tapati Mashi's madness was the reason for my mother's refusal to seek help. No one in our family wanted to face that we were cursed with madness. Where did the disdain for Tapati Mashi's mental illness come from? I can only assume the answer lies in history, a history that defined my family; in the colonial shadows that unconsciously shaded the psyches and households in Kolkata. Tapati Mashi's illness of the mind was terrifying for all to behold because it threatened to prove what the British had long described Indians to be—barbaric. A population that Winston Churchill once called 'a beastly people, with a beastly religion'. India, a sophisticated nation filled with artists, intellectuals, engineers and Nobel laureates, would—if it acknowledged any kind of mania—unintentionally admit that the British imperialists, who had long disdained brown men and women as primitive and uncivilized—their faith irrational, their tongues incoherent babbling—might be correct. For, what is more savage than madness?

I had thought my mother wanted to reach an accord, to return to the connection that we once had. Now, I felt broken by the knowledge that we would never heal, that I would remain hooked to a rubber band, forever expanding and contracting, lurching towards and away from my mother.

Mr Reyes was our constant witness, though he seemed helpless in the face of my mother's fury and averted his eyes to the floor. He never stood up to her, and part of me must have resented his failure to do so. I was angry that even he, the warmest and kindest of men, wouldn't challenge her behaviour. His failure, too, kept me away from LA.

On the day my mother lashed out after I broached therapy, Mr Reyes waited till she was nowhere to be found. Then, he came up to me and gently placed his hand on my shoulder, as if he believed I might shatter from any weight.

'I am sorry about the fight. You know your mother loves you.'

But I did not know she loved me.

I never brought up the subject of therapy with her again—I even forgot that it would help me.

WINTER 2015
DISCOVERY

BURNING WITH THE SHAME I felt at the hospital, I make it my mission to find out what has happened during the year my mother stayed under my Rima Mashi's care.

I learn that my mother's Parkinson's—combined with the sedatives presumably offered for her mental afflictions—made her sleep for hours at a time. Her bones had grown so brittle that she could barely move. Rima Mashi herself had other callings—she would travel to distant places—and at such times, my mother was without her supervision.

I wonder what this must have felt like to my mother—nothing to occupy her time but her hunger, the wetness of her own bodily fluids, her gaze on the ceiling and its travelling fan. I imagine my mother's body so infused with pain that pain became a normal state of being.

I visit my mother's bank in Kolkata and demand to see the statements. They show repeated withdrawals—but why? I don't understand it. I look down at the bank's floor and start sweating. The room falls forward as I feel vomit rising into my throat. I sit very still and focus on the objects scattered across the bank manager's desk—the old computer, the piles of papers. I remember my mother's days in Century 21, when the real estate market slowed and the office sat empty except for the clutter of flyers for houses that no one wanted to buy. As I wait at the bank manager's desk, I stiffen my throat and wrap an imaginary rope around my neck, waiting for the vomit to recede.

I go to speak to Rima Mashi to get a keener sense of the goings-on during my absence. I knock on the door. She slowly opens it.

There is no toothless smile this time. She trembles ever so slightly. I sit on the wooden couch in the living room, my back straight against its harsh, barely cushioned surface. The photos above us, housed in a hutch, show the trajectory of my mother and me—our love, our contentions—ending with who I am at this very moment—a child who desperately wants to save her mother, care for her, regardless of all the afflictions of the past, even while a part of her feels unable to.

I look at my Rima Mashi's face. Her glasses slide to the tip of her nose. Small bits of perspiration form on its bridge. 'Why didn't you hire a nurse?' I finally ask her.

'There was no need to. I took care of her,' she says. 'And do you know what your mother said to me? She took me to the bathroom and made me look in the mirror. *Who is prettier?* That is what she asked me. What do you think of that?' Her voice starts to rise.

'But why wasn't the withdrawn money used to hire someone?' I ask, as my hands begin to shake. I suddenly feel angry, I don't understand Rima Mashi's response, and I desperately want answers for my mother's demise. But is Rima Mashi the one to give me answers? My legs tense as I feel like lunging towards her. Then, my anger mutates into wonder. Why did my mother ask Rima Mashi who was prettier? Was jealousy really what lay beneath the events that had unfolded? Was the cause of all that my mother was going through the large black-and-white photo in my childhood bedroom, made by my Dida, to display her prettiest child, whom she loved more than any of the others, because she believed that the rest did not meet colonial standards of fairness?

My mother was supposed to save them all with her fair skin and large brown eyes. And when my mother didn't save them, she became nothing but a disappointment, another stain on the family name, a continuation of the disgrace that had begun with Tapati Mashi's madness.

Rima Mashi had once cared for me and fed me when no one else would. I now know that when my mother abandoned me and Rima Mashi had to adopt her role, the burden was just one more spoke in the wheel of resentment.

I also come to see the horrific nature of my mother's question to Rima Mashi. How, at sixty-eight, could my mother still ask such a thing, be so preoccupied with her appearance?

'Why are you telling me this now?' I ask my aunt.

But I see that the question is meaningless.

She has said what she had to. And now, there's no way of taking it back.

22

AFTER FINISHING MY TIME AT Boston College, I entered a PhD programme in Ethnic Studies at the University of California, Berkeley. I met a man with whom I fell deeply in love. We built a life together, with two small rescue dogs named Pablo and Devi, and in an adorable apartment furnished with blue curtains, a red armchair and a purple velvet couch that we bought from a local boutique store. We held parties on a deck, where I played hostess and fashioned myself in vintage dresses that I lined with plush petticoats. I bought these extravagant outfits from obscure thrift stores, thick, fake gold jewellery layering my neck. I wore four-inch heels that defined my calves. I painted my lips in burgundy, coral, sometimes gold and red. My cheekbones were accentuated with bronzer, my skin dusted with a golden shimmer, so I could sparkle as I walked about in the Californian sun.

When I see photos of myself from that time, I realize how much I was trying to emulate my mother's look from when she was a young woman—her '70s frocks and ornate sandals, the shoes in primary colours that lined the floor of her closet, the wardrobe that held rows of silk saris from her time in London during her twenties—sunshine yellow, magenta, forest green. As a little girl, I'd loved tracing my fingers over all her clothes or climbing up her body to see the different shades she carried on her face. I wanted to be that bright woman she had been before becoming a real estate agent, before she realized the need to assimilate, before her clothes became drab and boring.

A few years into my relationship, I found out that my partner had been cheating on me. My relationship had kept me safe from my mother and my belief that I wasn't good enough to be loved. But now, my self-made family was falling apart. I had gone to school, done well and was on my way to being an academic; yet, even though I had become a proper girl, nobody wanted me.

I looked for an escape from the pain of my partner's betrayal by forming a reliance on alcohol, cocaine and clonazepam, which a doctor had prescribed for my restlessness. I took the clonazepam every day in higher and higher doses to ease my anxiety; no amount ever seemed to be enough. I did not turn to my mother for comfort, but I felt the young girl inside of me who wanted to climb out, call her mother and have a normal conversation filled with motherly reassurance.

Ma, am I going to be all right?

Ha, sona, you will be, I promise.

I lost weight and people noticed. 'You look sick,' they said. 'Are you eating?'

I wasn't.

I had completed my exams for my doctorate and the next thing to do was finish my dissertation. I pushed that aside. I travelled instead to the house clubs in the Castro, high on cocaine, and to the EndUp every Sunday for tea dance, embracing it as my church. I begged the gods of house music: *Soothe my soul, bless my heart, make this agony go away, and find someone to love me.*

But then, my skin responded to the heartbreak. My cystic acne returned with fury. Each cyst was hard and round, the size of a nickel. I slathered my skin with Retin-A and rubbing alcohol, hoping to burn each spot off. But the spots didn't go away. Instead, they became a cartography of open wounds, a blueprint of my melancholy. I felt hyper-visible, as if I was a cartoon living amongst the real.

The last time I had felt the urge to mutilate myself was when Aarush had broken my heart. That compulsion returned with angst.

One day, I could not stop going to my bathroom to inspect each bump. I went to the mirror and touched the raised red skin that was throbbing on my right cheekbone. I reached for a needle inside my medicine cabinet and lit a match to its tip; it glowed. Then, I placed the needle in the middle of the hard lump and forced it in, hoping to extract whatever it was that made me ache. Nothing came out.

I decided that the compulsion and the repeated trips to the mirror had to stop. I poured whiskey into a vintage tumbler collected from one of the various thrift stores I frequented. It was decorated in gold maple leaves, and its surface was smooth in comparison to my skin. I looked down into it, sniffed the sharp bite of alcohol and took a sip. My eyes moved towards the bottle of clonazepam on my bedside table. I grabbed the container and pushed the fleshy part of my palm into the childproof lid to turn it open. I grabbed what was left, my teeth chomping some of the pills into a sea green slush. I wiggled a few under my tongue and waited for them to dissolve. I was an expert at taking benzos, and knew that if used sublingually, the drug would enter my bloodstream faster. I let my head fall to my pillow. I kept my eyes open but saw nothing as I waited to feel the lull of sedation.

I don't know how many minutes passed before I began to feel woozy. I looked down at the length of my bed. Devi was cuddling the inside of my legs, Pablo was curled into a tight fluffy bun next to her. I imagined them orphaned and confused, just like the day my mother had left me in India. Instinctually and without panic, I reached for my rose-coloured flip phone. My fingers slowly pushed each button until a friend's voice was on the other end of the line. She lived a few blocks away and had a key to my apartment. My legs felt like barbells, sinking into my mattress as I tried to get out of bed. I moved like a sloth, sluggishly shifting my feet off the bedside, my head trailing away from my pillow, my hair spread across the cream sheets like an accordion fan.

I saw the shadow of my friend behind the sheer curtain of my front door. She opened the door and found me on the bed, my legs hanging off the side. She ran towards me, cupping her hands beneath my armpits and leading me to the toilet, where she forced her hand into my mouth. As she tickled my throat, my stomach pulsed like a heart. Whatever was inside of me fell out of my mouth, mint green foam dissolving with toilet water.

My friend told me that if I didn't see a therapist, she would have to take me to the emergency room and tell them about the pills, the alcohol, the mutilation of my face and my inability to sleep. I would be held against my will for seventy-two hours.

I also knew that if I didn't do something, my ulcerated mind would begin to kill me.

The next day, I visited the mental health centre at Berkeley to see a psychiatrist. She was a white woman with wheat-coloured hair. She sat across me in a buttery black leather chair; it looked so comfortable, as if it were a psychiatric throne. She held a notebook and scribbled things as I told her about the night before, but I didn't tell her everything. I didn't want to be held captive at an asylum like my Tapati Mashi.

'So, tell me, is there any history of depression in your family?' she asked.

It was such a profound question. To *name* our family's afflictions. Was depression the right word? Did it encompass all the violence?

'Well, my mother is mentally ill, but she has never been diagnosed. She doesn't really believe in Western medicine. She has pretty bad mood swings,' I replied.

The psychiatrist crossed her legs. 'And tell me about your compulsions. What does it feel like when you want to pick at your face?'

I told her how I couldn't control my body's movements. My body acted without my consent and repeatedly led me to the bathroom. I couldn't concentrate on anything but the agony in my face, of whatever was bubbling under the surface, as if the layers of my skin had become my unconscious and my psyche was boiling.

Within twenty minutes, the psychiatrist diagnosed me with OCD and depression. She gave me some Lexapro and told me that the medication would make me feel better in a few weeks.

I never saw the psychiatrist again. Suddenly, on the Lexapro, I no longer felt the pain of lost lovers or the heartache of betrayal—I felt manic. I gained sixty-five pounds and euphoria saturated everything I did. I was filled with want. I had the drive of an infant or toddler with no impulse control, gnawing and reaching for every object I desired. I went out even more frequently and my interest in my dissertation fell completely to the wayside.

Unconsciously, I thought about my family's past and how my mother's history must have written my future; how it led me to the moment when I had to sit in a psychiatrist's office and finally ask for help.

23

WHEN I TURNED THIRTY, MY mother made me marry a plant. She said that if I married one, I would find true love.

Two years before, I had been standing in front of twelve students in a first-year writing seminar at Vassar College, explaining Freud's theory of mourning and melancholia. I had run away from my life at Berkeley, thinking a predoctoral position at Vassar would help me finish my dissertation on the trauma of India's Partition. I felt powerful before new students and young minds, and thought I was going to mould them, even enlighten them with my brilliance. They all stared at me, photocopied essays of Freud's 'Fetishism' in their hands, nervous to be in a completely new environment. I was not. I was on a manic high from the Lexapro that the psychiatrist at Berkeley had prescribed; the drug made me feel fearless. Later, a psychiatrist would tell me that many people who are bipolar react to a SSRIs (which Lexapro was) with mania; that I was bipolar, not simply anxious and depressed. I now had something akin to an answer for my actions.

I continued to delve into books about the psychic nature of loss as I tried to write my dissertation. I thought of my mother and Dida every time I picked up one of the novels I taught—Amitav Ghosh's *The Shadow Lines*, Bapsi Sidhwa's *Cracking India*, Maxine Hong Kingston's *The Woman Warrior*, Toni Morrison's *The Bluest Eye* and Jhumpa Lahiri's *Interpreter of Maladies*. I was becoming an interpreter of maladies myself. I interrogated my Dida's fixation with whiteness. Her treatment of her daughters based on their skin colour and gender always lingered at the back of my mind as I spoke to students about race, the impact of centuries of imperial rule and the powerfully articulated theories of scholars such as Frantz Fanon on the unconscious effects of colonialism. I saw how the mechanisms of colonization had infiltrated my Dida's psyche. A colonized mind means that, in part, colonialism has worked. It has achieved its physical and psychic purpose—the notion that you are less than, or even worse, monstrous, sleeps in a dark, hidden part of you. You integrate the belief; it nests comfortably inside your unconscious. Your consciousness fights the unconscious in an ongoing battle. The results can be violent.

When I explained Cathy Caruth's theory of the inability to register trauma—about how we are incapable of translating psychic pain into language—I thought about my mother's refusal to name her afflictions, her repudiation of anything being wrong with her. Perhaps the trauma of our family's past cannot be captured by language. And here I was, trying to articulate all that trauma and pain through an academic lexicon.

Meanwhile, on the Lexapro, I craved all things pleasurable, as I had when I'd entered the throes of puberty. The girl who preferred being a famous academic to having an exciting sex life fell away from me. I rabidly consumed food to soak up all the vodka I drank each night. I went out into Poughkeepsie or took the train to New York City so I could find strangers to fuck. I had sex with women and men in bathrooms and in my car. My first time with a woman, I put my tongue on her clit and felt the slippery-slick wetness, the warmth, the sharp taste of her inner being. I stuck one, two, three fingers inside of her. I made her moan from the force of my fingers, my tickling of her insides. I thought of my mother and the day that she'd shown me her vagina.

I would drive home while inebriated. Once, at a DUI checkpoint, I drunkenly approached the officer at the stop sign and batted my long eyelashes thick with mascara, my lips bright red.

'Hi, officer, what is going on?'

'Where have you been tonight, miss?'

He glanced at my hands, which were braced on the steering wheel, to see if I was wearing a ring. There was a small smirk on his face as his eyes moved to my collarbone and then my plunging neckline; my breasts were now full and large from the weight I had gained.

'Oh, I teach at Vassar. I was just at a colleague's house for dinner.'

The dry remains of cum on my hands reminded me that I was lying.

'I see. Well, get home safe.'

The colour of my skin, not as fair as my Dida desired but still light, was a privilege when I encountered the police. I wasn't subjected to the extreme and brutal violence Black men and women are. I was able to use my sexuality the way my mother had when she was young. Just as she had, I flaunted my sex and skin to my advantage. But using my body did not deliver me what she and I wanted most—love.

My time at Vassar was painfully chequered; it was a lesson in how the cloistered community of a liberal arts college can be as cruel and gossipy as my Dida's neighbourhood in Kolkata. They were both spaces where people whispered about my behaviour, noticed what time I came home and talked about my mental health. One faculty member, famous for his liberal politics and beloved by students, told people that I wasn't right in the head.

I wasn't.

My sexual appetite was the biggest problem. I lived across the street from the front gates of the campus. The size of the school was so small that everyone knew what everyone's car looked like. When people came over and parked in my lot overnight, colleagues noticed. Faculty members asked me, 'Whose car was at your house?'

I never had sex with anyone at school, only people I met outside the gates that separated the people who belonged to Vassar and the people who did not.

When the faculty members rejected me, I made friends with a couple of students. One, a girl named Lilia, became my constant companion. She had long, straight black hair, plush lips, wide brown eyes, and a large bosom that drew men and women's eyes towards her. She was half-Asian, half-white. You could see her mixed-race heritage in her skin, eyes and hair. Or I could. My eyes were trained to recognize those who were like me; I investigated faces, searching for reflections of my biracial heritage. I was Lilia's thesis advisor during her senior year at Vassar, and we developed a connection that survived long after she graduated. Our friendship was a sisterhood while it lasted. I confided in her during my time at Vassar. She helped me to survive the shame of being an outcast in a village that rejected me and my mania.

But I was her professor. There was a power imbalance in our relationship. I was twenty-eight, and I should have known that I was at Vassar not to confide in the twenty-one-year-old students, but to advise.

I was a problem, and therefore, I had to be shunned. At parties, when I would approach my colleagues to engage in conversation, they would walk away from me. The professors would look at me the way the girls at my school in Kolkata once had—the girls who knew how to be good and appropriate, how to study, how not to spread their legs before marriage. I wanted to learn to be proper, too. I wanted someone to tell me why I behaved in the ways that I did, and why my behaviour was beyond my mind's control.

I searched for a therapist and began seeing him twice a week—a sophisticated man who had been trained in psychoanalysis in New York City. I looked up to him and followed his directions. He thought it was best that I get off the Lexapro, so I did. It wasn't hard to wean myself off the drug because, all at once, I was in love with my therapist—Freud's theory of transference wasn't untrue. I redirected all the emotions I had for my mother, my dead father and lost lovers onto him. He became a new drug, allowing me to interpret my malaise and not just the historical backdrop that had forged my family. I shifted away from academese and chronicled my life as though telling a folktale. I immersed myself in the amniotic blanket of the talking cure.

I received my PhD in 2007 and was about to start a lecturing position at Harvard University. I was sad to be leaving my therapist but grateful to be leaving Vassar. As I walked across the stage at Berkeley to receive my degree, moving the tassel of my cap from left to right, I looked out into the auditorium to search for my mother. I found her. Her hair was dyed jet-black and tied into a messy bun. Her signature bobby pins lined her hairline. Her eyes met mine, and her smile was wide. I think I saw an expression of pride on her face. Perhaps she'd smiled this wide when I was born, happy to have someone she could mould, someone who would grow to love her unconditionally.

My mother had been consulting holy men about my fate, her fate, Mr Reyes's fate. With each passing year, her reliance on astrologers and prophets grew stronger. She followed their directions and only took trips during the times they had designated as safe. They asked her for money, which she had now, thanks to Mr Reyes. She did not have to ration for travel the way she did when I was young and she needed to make the inheritance my father left us last.

My graduation came only a few weeks before my thirtieth birthday, and my mother was deeply concerned that I was unmarried. She begged me to come home and perform a ritual she believed would solve the problem of my spinsterhood.

From what I could ascertain, I was to marry a plant.

My soon-to-be husband peeked above the edges of a tiny terracotta pot—a basil plant that had barely sprouted, as if only just entering the throes of puberty. He sat next to a brass votive candle with a tiny glint of flame—the fire deity.

During my nuptials, no trails of smoke spiralled up through the air like the lines of fate. Instead, the ceremony was held in our television room in Los Angeles—a large Panasonic flatscreen providing a backdrop. The television was turned off, so nothing could distract from the importance of the moment.

Though I thought my mother's growing superstitions were alarming, I now know why I agreed to perform the ritual that day. I was trained to be a nuanced academic. My life's goal was to educate young minds on how the developing world was not the poverty-ridden, archaic space that the media often represented. I challenged my students to redefine terms like 'primitive', 'provincial' and 'backward'. The early nineteenth century's 'civilizing mission' identified reason with the West and irrationality with the East. I wanted my students to interrogate this history, to think about what it meant to be 'sophisticated' and 'cultured'. When they spoke of a regressive East, I asked—wasn't the Victorian practice that brides wear white a perpetuation of the idea that a woman must be pure, innocent and virginal? I knew *all* rituals were about kinship and culture, the creation of memories in order to forge bonds and construct identity. On the day of my marriage to the plant, I believed I'd conceded to my mother's desire because I was seeking an understanding of a world, I was trying to bridge cultural difference. I also hoped to understand more deeply my mother's beliefs. Still, while the ceremony unfolded, I could not help but feel the whole affair was ridiculous.

A decade after my plant-marriage, I finally researched the meaning of my matrimony. I asked academic friends and looked online, until I found out I was a 'manglik'—a victim of an astrological condition in which Mars's position in the ascendant chart signals marital misfortune or an inability to find a partner. A remedy is 'kumbh vivah'—marrying a banyan or banana tree—a majestic plant whose roots crawl across the earth and whose branches stretch through the sky. A shallow understanding of this ritual states that all the troubles are transferred to the tree and the curse is then lifted; one is free to find a suitable partner. I discovered the practice was not uncommon—no more obscure than taking the sacrament or a bris.

At the end of the service, an astrologer tied a string around my wrist—thin slivers of red and white intertwined. As weeks went by, I watched the bracelet grow dirty, the white turning beige, then brown. I fiddled with the threads during conversations with friends and strangers. I rolled them between my fingers and felt my bond with the small plant that was my partner, invisible but symbolic. I let time and friction run their course, until one day, the string fell off. I wondered: *now will I meet someone to love me?*

This desire to be loved was the other reason I had agreed to the marriage that day. I secretly hoped the ceremony would soothe my heartbreak and deliver me someone who'd cherish me for who I was. I was my mother's child; how could I not have inherited some of her beliefs? I think I may have even quietly assumed that she was a fortune-teller. My subconscious always wondered if her practices would yield the outcomes she craved.

Even as I tried to ignore my mother's blind faith in astrologers, I could not help but notice that Mr Reyes was losing hold of his memory.

One night, Mr Reyes woke me, the sound of his feet searching the cold marble floor as he roamed the house. I got out of bed and followed the murmurs of his rummaging. He was going through the contents of his desk drawer.

'Dad, are you okay?' I asked, rubbing my eyes.

'Yes, honey. Have you seen my keys?'

'It's the middle of the night. Where are you going?' I asked.

'I need to get some milk for the cereal.'

'Dad, it's three in the morning.'

'Oh, for some reason I thought it was already morning. I must have had a dream where it was.'

'Okay, why don't you go back to sleep?'

'Thanks, honey, I will.'

I knew the man who had treated me like a daughter was in danger. It was clear to me that Mr Reyes was probably developing Alzheimer's and should be on some sort of medication. I could sense that my mother's refusal to take him to a doctor was partly a form of neglect.

Instead of confronting my mother or taking Mr Reyes to an allopath, I ignored the bewildered look on his face. I didn't want to be around my mother, so I disregarded what was happening.

There were so many times that Mr Reyes had looked away from my mother's fury; was I doing the same thing to him? Was I ignoring his failing health because he had failed to protect me from my mother's wrath? Was I privileging my own mental health at the expense of my parents' lives?

Yet, I also couldn't deny the fact that I feared my mother's rage—the combustible gas stove that lived within her. I lied to myself and thought—*surely, she will take care of him*—though she had never taken care of anyone, including herself. I did not want to run into the house on fire. I wanted to save myself, even if it meant that someone I loved would be left, burning.

24

DURING THE FINANCIAL CRISIS OF 2008, my mother began to sell off Mr Reyes's property, purchasing homes in India because she thought the banks in the United States were failing. She dragged Mr Reyes around the world, much as she had done with me when I was a child. Each time they returned to their large home in Pasadena, she returned with a man whose brain was getting more decimated by an illness that destroys the very thing that makes us human—our histories and stories. She must have felt utterly alone.

My mother liquidated her assets and, as recession gutted the country, she made a mad dash to buy gold coins, burying them in the backyard. She began to give astrologers and godmen piles of cash if they promised to keep her safe from death, disease and poverty. Some of her actions may have been appropriate responses to the financial catastrophes that were befalling the nation, but something in the cadence of her speech, the pitch of each syllable, hinted to me that her panic wasn't a natural reaction to the times alone.

In his younger days, Mr Reyes had been a tall man, his shoulders wide; when he walked into a room his presence was impossible to ignore. He had had thick hair that went from jet-black to steely grey, yet never receded. But in the years before my Dida's death, he had become frail, his shoulders hunched, his frame thinner.

Whenever I encountered my mother and Mr Reyes, I felt a rush of panic. I wanted to convince my mother that selling property, burying gold in the backyard and buying houses in India were overreactions. But trying to persuade her was pointless. When I called and begged her to take Mr Reyes to a doctor, to get him the medication he needed, her only response was, 'I know what I am doing.'

It had been four years since I had visited India. I was beginning to miss Kolkata and my childhood friend Ritwik and his mother Kabita. Ritwik and I had always kept in touch. My former student from Vassar, Lilia, who had, over time, become like my younger sister, had never been to India and wanted to go with me.

I told Lilia that my mother could be violent. 'We shouldn't go when she is there,' I warned her. I don't think she believed me.

We decided to go in the summer. It was only a few months after my graduation—the perfect time to visit, in my eyes, because I would be away from my mother, who only visited Kolkata during the winter, when she and Mr Reyes liked to travel the world.

Two weeks before Lilia and I were to depart, I was sitting at my kitchen table trying to turn my dissertation into a book—something I urgently needed to do to make myself more competitive in the academic job market. I stared at my computer screen, hoping that letters would magically appear and sprint their way into sentences. A blank page glared at me with defiance.

My cell phone began to vibrate. I usually ignored my mother's calls. But when the phone rang for the third time, the desperation of each vibration indicated I needed to answer.

'Haan, Ma,' I said.

'She's dead. Your Dida is dead. My mother is dead. I am going to Kolkata tonight.'

I felt nothing, no pang of longing or grief. My mind felt blank, as if I had developed amnesia. Then, I worried that I would have to see my mother while I was in India.

'Why are you going? I don't get it. She was always mean to you,' I said, as my legs began to shake.

'She is my mother. I have to go,' she replied.

'Fine. Do what you need to.'

My words whistled with dismissiveness. I didn't care that my Dida was dead. I was insensitive to my mother's pain and panic. I didn't realize that the loss of a mother can be the biggest loss of all, no matter the hurt she might have inflicted.

Lilia and I arrived in Kolkata two weeks after my Dida's death. My mother was at the airport to pick us up. Standing next to Mr Reyes, waiting for us to collect our luggage from the carousel, she looked delicate and fragile from loss. When she reached out to embrace me, my skin tightened as it always did, and a tiny streak of vomit moved up my throat. I swallowed it back down. As usual, my mother felt my disgust and hardened. My repudiation of her brand of motherly love was too much for her to bear in the face of the loss of her own mother. I felt the mean girl from my younger years flaring up. I looked around and watched other people embracing their loved ones with ease and tenderness. I wished I could experience the same happiness they did—the happiness that comes from seeing a family member after too long away. Instead, what I felt was anger, and when I hoisted my luggage off the baggage carousel, each wheel on the floor released a tiny tornado of dust.

My mother turned her attention to Lilia. Her eyes narrowed, and I could see now that she viewed my friend as an imposition, someone with whom I wanted to spend time when she wanted me all to herself.

My mother was sixty years old. I was thirty, the same age my mother was when she gave birth to me. My skin was tanned from days of going to the beaches on Cape Cod and the North Shore of Massachusetts.

'You're too dark. You look dirty,' my mother said, as she studied me. For a moment, I felt overwhelming shame at the colour of my skin and wanted my mother's fair complexion.

Lilia was aware of the tension between us and remained quiet by my side as we walked to a taxi and drove to a house my mother had purchased in a small Ayurvedic village two hours outside the city. We arrived at a two-storey cottage next to a muddy stream in the middle of an oasis of homes. I had never seen the house before because I had ignored how she had been handling Mr Reyes's estate. But I knew she wanted to return to the country where she had been born and that she wanted to die there; the cottage was the first step in her departure.

We were supposed to stay with my mother five days—two days past my usual limit—before driving to Kolkata, where we would stay with Kabita. During our first few days, Lilia and I explored the compounds. Vedic Village was a gated community, with a guard at the entrance who kept out the poor of the surrounding town. The grounds reminded me of Vassar, where a guard sat at a similar checkpoint and scanned IDs to keep out the mostly Black community of Poughkeepsie. A bright blue pool shaped like a lotus sat in the centre of the Ayurvedic village. Two restaurants and a tiny office with old computers connected to Ethernet cables stood adjacent to the pool. Lilia and I checked our email every few hours, trying to escape the boredom of being far away from the bustling city.

As we investigated the property, I grew acutely aware of how Lilia looked and dressed, the way her clothes exposed her breasts and how the men stared at her. I felt protective of Lilia. Even before we had left the US, I had told her that customs were different in Kolkata. 'I think you should bring some shirts that are a little discreet,' I had said.

'Okay, but isn't it going to be hot? I don't really have anything to wear but my tank tops.'

Lilia was a Brooklyn hipster of the 2000s who wore jean shorts, low-cut tank tops and ankle boots, garments that felt incongruous against the saris and kurtas of Vedic Village.

Even as I warned Lilia to cover herself in Kolkata, I felt a sense of shame, a failure as a feminist who couldn't allow her to do as she pleased with her body. But when I visited India, I wanted to stay within the boundaries of being a good girl, because I wanted to make up for my past reputation as a bad girl. I was also an academic who knew that cultural context was crucial.

'We should just try and go by how they do things in Kolkata, you know? Even if we don't agree.'

Confused, Lilia left the solution up to me. I found a remedy. I let Lilia borrow some of my mother's shirts; her kurtas fit Lilia perfectly, even if they clashed with her style. Lilia accepted the compromise, though I could tell she felt uncomfortable.

I had not asked my mother if I could borrow her belongings and lend them to a girl she barely knew. I didn't connect my action to the day I had taken my father's tapes without permission and the rage I had ignited. Although, maybe, on some level, I did know that borrowing those shirts would infuriate my mother.

A day or two into our stay at my mother's cottage, I visited the business centre by myself, checked my email and lingered around the pool. Lilia remained in the house, wanting to rest under the fan in her bedroom. I hadn't been privy to a Kolkata summer since I was a child, so I had forgotten just how hot it got, the block of humidity that made you sweat as if your body were an open faucet. I walked through the dense air and sat at the edge of the pool, dipping each of my feet into the electric blue water. I examined my skin and the orange of my nail polish. I wanted to dip my entire body into the pool and rinse off my colour, swim to the bottom, touch the cement and find the sadness I wasn't able to feel about my Dida's death. I suddenly realized I had been sitting there for a long time and needed to get back to Lilia. I walked towards my mother's cottage, pool water trickling off my legs.

When I arrived, I could hear my mother's voice rising as she shouted at Lilia.

'Why are you wearing my things? Don't you know it's dirty and unhealthy to borrow?'

I quickly walked up the stairs to the second floor. The dryer was on, a load of laundry going around with a wallop each time it hit the bottom of a cycle. I found my mother and Lilia near the top of the stairwell, my mother's hand wrapped firmly around Lilia's wrist. Lilia looked pale and in a stupor; she did not know how to react to my mother's anger. She was wearing one of my mother's kurtas.

'She is a bad girl,' my mother said, as she turned towards me. Then she began to furiously shake Lilia, whose head bobbled as if it had just popped out of a jack-in-the-box.

I knew how strong my mother could be, even at sixty. I reached for her arm, but her hands clasped Lilia. I could not prise open her grip. So, I pushed my mother up the stairs, until she finally let go of Lilia.

Soon after, we entered the room I slept in. There was an empty space that ran across the bottom of the bedroom wall.

I looked through the gap at the living room below and saw myself falling to the ground, breaking my neck or my skull, a stream of black blood pooled around my head. My fantasies were always that—a fall would permanently remove me from the living.

Lilia backed into the corner of the room, away from my mother. This is when I fully registered what my mother looked like. Her hair was in two braids. No bobby pins hid her balding spots. Her face was warped like twisted metal. I saw in her a sadness that came from the loss of my Dida and a rage that was being fanned by the failing electrical wires of her brain, sparks flying from each tip.

A nervous smile slowly crept across Lilia's face. This infuriated my mother even more. The veins on the sides of her forehead hammered, blue-grey metronomes.

'You think this is funny!' my mother yelled. 'You are a terrible girl.'

Lilia's laugh became louder. I wanted to laugh, too. How else could we react to a woman who had become hysterical because someone had borrowed her shirt?

My mother moved her arm towards Lilia's ear, her thumb and index finger ready to pull it. Before I realized what I was doing, I had blocked my mother's advance, dug my hands into her chest and pushed her away. She began to stumble and raised her arms to regain her balance, to steady her wobbling body. She was grasping the air around her to find something to hold on to. Her hands searched for me to give her equilibrium.

'I can't see!' she yelled. 'There are things around me!'

My rage created an impenetrable wall of steel, a pure defence against my mother, her screams, her vulnerability, her blindness. I did not reach out to her to offer her balance. I did not care if she collapsed to the floor, if her head hit the cold tiles, if she died right there.

'I can't see anything!' she repeated.

My mother had never literally gone blind from her rage. I could tell that something strange was happening to her—something biological rather than psychological. But I didn't care. Her blindness was our freedom. I turned towards Lilia and said, 'Let's go,' even though I had no idea how to get to the city without my mother's rental car.

I called Kabita and asked if we could stay with her. She could hear the panic in my voice and said yes. I pulled my clothes from the armoire and stuffed them into my handbag. Lilia was in her room doing the same thing. I tried to plot our escape—find someone to take us on a bicycle or an autorickshaw; hire the taxi we needed to get to the city—but I didn't know how to begin the journey.

I heard Mr Reyes climbing the stairs.

'What is going on?' he asked.

'Your wife is being crazy,' I responded. I had never referred to my mother as anything other than my mother. But on that day, I renounced her as my parent, not dignifying her with her title, 'Ma'.

Mr Reyes looked at me with marbly cataract eyes, unable to respond. He stood next to my mother, confused.

While we packed, my mother searched my room with blinking eyes, trying to reorient herself with her surroundings.

'I will take you to the city,' she said.

I don't exactly know why I allowed my mother to drive us. Maybe the only way to get away from her was to let her be our chariot to freedom. I can't recall if my mother yelled the whole way or if we all sat in silence. I know Mr Reyes was not with us. We had carelessly left him behind, forgetting just how fragile he had become. Suddenly, we arrived at a Fabindia store, where my mother had bought the kurtas I let Lilia borrow.

'What are we doing here?' I asked.

'I am going to get this girl some kurtas,' my mother responded.

As we got out of the car, my mother suddenly reached for Lilia's hand and dragged her into the shop, barging her way in. I tried to catch up. She stopped in the middle of the store and began to pull kurtas off shelves, patterns of paisley, batik and dabu interspersed with solid shades of royal blue, coral and rust.

'Here, pick one!' my mother yelled. Women seeking saris stopped and stared. I was immobile, frozen by how utterly embarrassing this moment was.

Lilia stepped backwards, pressing herself into a row of shirts neatly folded on a wooden shelf.

At the time, I didn't recognize that I had created this scene. I had allowed my mother's violence to boil over onto another person. Lilia had been like a sister to me, and a sibling is often the only witness to a parent's abuse; I *needed* an observer who could confirm my mother's violence and verify that I had not made up my childhood. Because, until that moment, my mother had been like Schrödinger's cat—she was simultaneously the good mother she told herself she was and the bad mother I believed her to be.

My mother continued to yell, 'Pick one, you dirty girl!'

Lilia finally responded calmly, 'I don't want anything from you.'

The sound of Lilia's voice allowed me to move. I grabbed her hand and led her out of the store. My mother followed. I looked back and saw sweat trickling down my mother's forehead, mingling with the kajol in her eyes. Streaks of black bisected her cheeks. She began to follow us.

When we got to the road, a taxi driver was leaning against his yellow Ambassador and smoking a bidi. I gave him Kabita's address. As Lilia and I jumped into his car, my mother began to reach for my hand, but she couldn't catch me.

When we eventually reached Kabita's house, she welcomed us and led us to Ritwik's childhood room; Ritwik was away. The room held many memories of my time in Kolkata, where I had made friends who loved me. Ritwik's artwork was all over—splashes of primary red, yellow and blue on large canvases that stretched across like wallpaper. A small bed and a thin extra mattress lay in one corner, and this is where Lilia and I slept for the remainder of our trip. I let Lilia sleep on the bed because I was ashamed of my mother's violence. It was my fault that I had taken my mother's clothes without asking, and thus I had subjected Lilia to her attack.

That first night with Kabita, I went to the bathroom and looked out of a tiny window. It was night, and the sound of cars beeping rang in my eardrums. The air was obese; it cradled me with newfound emotion. I slipped down to the floor, letting gravity take its course. I felt the strain of tears. I cried for the loss of my mother and my Dida—for, on that day, I promised myself I would never speak to my mother again, even while I knew that the promise would be impossible to keep.

25

IT WAS MY MOTHER'S SIXTY-SECOND birthday. I had not spoken to her for more than six hundred days.

The phone kept ringing, a long number that flashed across my iPhone screen, indicating it was a call from India. I didn't answer. A fourth and fifth call badgered me. I realized something must actually be wrong. I picked up the phone and didn't need to say anything.

'Rani. *Ami Rima Mashi*. Your Ma is going for surgery! Something has happened to her eye. She cannot open it. She wants to talk to you. You must come here!'

She handed the phone to my mother. I inhaled, as I expected to hear her normal voice, one I had not heard for two years … but I had never heard my mother's voice carry such pangs of panic.

'Rani! Help me! I don't know what is wrong. I don't want to have surgery. What is happening, my eye won't open!' The Bengali accent she had hidden during the years she had tried to assimilate into American society now fully emerged. She didn't sound like my mother—the alarm and accent intertwined. I felt a lump in my throat like an Adam's apple, air turning into a mass of fear. I had no choice but to give in to my mother, the frightened woman who lay in a hospital at the other end of the earth.

'Ma,' I said, 'it's okay, it's going to be okay.'

While I had not spoken to my mother in two years, she had reached out through emails, letters and voice messages. I was so firm in my decision never to speak to her again that I hadn't responded. My relationship with Lilia had dwindled to occasional texts and false promises to hang out and catch up. I was embarrassed by my mother's behaviour and the possibility that I had intentionally exposed Lilia to risk. That day on the phone, though, when I heard my mother's terror, all my anger got siphoned away.

I can't explain why I broke my promise to never speak to her again. I wonder why it was so easy for me to let go, momentarily, of all my anger and resentment. It must have been our quantum entanglement—unexplainable, mysterious but nevertheless true.

When I called the next morning, Rima Mashi handed my mother the phone.

'Hehehehehehe, shourowugn ourksutipbhsm.'

'What is wrong?' I demanded of my mother.

She responded with laughter eerily similar to my Tapati Mashi's. My hand gripped my phone. I wanted to crush it, crack its screen, feel the glass shards puncture my skin.

Rima Mashi took the phone away from my mother.

'What is wrong with her?' I asked.

'She is going to be fine. Yes, yes. Fine, fine.'

Her irrational assertion prickled my mind. 'What are you talking about? She's speaking nonsense.'

'No, no, this is okay, believe in bhagavan, he will make all good.'

My family's irrationality has always made me feel like I am boiling in something thick and sticky, a blob of scalding liquid threatening to consume my sanity. When I heard the ridiculousness of her words, my mind smarted.

But then, the small child in me—the one who rushed to her mother's side when she heard voices after one of her manic, rageful moments—appeared.

Whether it was her madness or mine, I knew I had to run back into the burning house and get my mother help.

Ritwik and his mother were at the airport to pick me up when I arrived in Kolkata a few days later. I had so much to do, and Ritwik knew it. I needed to make sure my mother got the care she needed and check in on Mr Reyes, who was now caught in the throes of Alzheimer's.

We swerved through Kolkata traffic and made our way to my Dida's old flat. When Rima Mashi opened the door to the flat that my mother had inherited, but that Rima Mashi now lived in, she smiled at us. Her toothless grin seemed more frightening than ever before, her hair grey and greasy from an abundance of coconut oil. Five years before, my mother had found Rima Mashi alone, with a fever from malaria. My mother had taken her to Dida's flat and nursed her back to health. Now, Rima Mashi was caring for my mother.

I walked to my childhood room and saw my mother sitting on the bed. Long stitches edged her hairline where bobby pins had once resided. Her left eyelid drooped downwards. Her face looked uneven and odd, not the symmetrical appearance that had once been both an asset and a liability to her. She giggled like a child, her grey hair plastered to her sweaty skin. She spoke to me in gibberish—incomprehensible words like the goo-goo-gah-gah of a newborn baby.

'Hi, Ma, I am here.'

I couldn't help the tears that fell from my eyes—for the person before me was not my mother. Ritwik held my hand. His touch was sturdy yet gentle, like the velvety feel of a rose, offering assurance and recognition of my mother's condition. No bhagavan—no god—could save her.

For the next few days, I travelled between Ritwik's mother's house and my Dida's flat to spend time with my mother. I read Jhumpa Lahiri's short stories to her while she lay in bed. She laughed at all the sad parts, opened her eyes with wonder at the parts that were banal. She did not know what I was saying or what the stories were about. I read to her anyway. During this time, Reyes sat in the living room staring at the wall, not knowing where he was, not knowing what to do. We mirrored each other, for I did not know what to do either.

I took my mother to the doctor to get an MRI. The doctor told me she had suffered a ruptured brain aneurysm and needed a few months before she could fly. I developed a schedule of tasks that needed to be done. I had a semester off from teaching while I was on a fellowship at Yale. I was still supposed to be writing my academic book, but that had to wait.

I returned to the United States and asked my parents' neighbours in California, who had been collecting their mail, to send all of it to me. I was worried about bills and other logistics that needed tending to. When the mail arrived, I found an urgent letter from the bank—'You have not paid your mortgage in four months. Your house will begin foreclosure.'

I frantically called the bank.

'You must pay four thousand dollars immediately, and it must be a cashier's check, otherwise we will foreclose on the house.'

I cashed out all my savings, paid the bank and made plans to fly to California to sort out my parents' affairs.

Something about the rush of a crisis forces you into a runner's stance, poised to move forward, your body fixed in a lunge, leaning towards the direction you need to sprint in.

And then you run.

My parents' bills had piled up, and each one read PAST DUE. Had they planned for such a contingency? Had they left papers that gave me power of attorney during a crisis? A health directive? The right to do what needed to be done when they were incapacitated and in need of help?

On the first day I was in Pasadena, I ransacked their house, pulling clothes out my mother's closet—salwar kameezes, her colourful saris from when she was young. I looked under the mountains of vitamins in the corners of the house; dug through stale herbs scattered in plastic bottles. I found files and documents in the kitchen cupboards, and pored through them, cha- and muri-stained papers that held nothing but Ayurvedic charts and drawings of yoga postures. My mother hated it when I touched her things without asking; now, my fingerprints were all over her belongings. When I was desperate, I remembered that my mother had said she had gold in the backyard, so I took a small shovel and started digging around the thin trunks of the avocado and lemon trees, to no avail. Looking up at the green and yellow fruit waiting to be plucked, half-blinded by the starfish rays of the Californian sunshine, I felt ridiculous. What was I doing digging up dirt? Did I really think I'd recover buried treasure?

A friend recommended an attorney, who told me I had to become my parents' conservator in order to take care of their affairs. I hired him and was granted a temporary conservatorship of my parents' estate, which meant I had control of their finances—but the court did not grant me temporary conservatorship of their health, a separate form of guardianship in which one has control of another's free will. I could only pay their bills and ensure they weren't financially vulnerable. Permanent conservatorship would be granted only when my parents returned to California, and when their acumen and bodily capacity could be assessed.

It took three plane rides and two layovers to get my parents back to California. During our sixteen-hour flight from Kolkata to Dubai, Mr Reyes stared at the air around him and periodically asked, 'Why is this building flying?'

I walked him down the narrow aisles of the double-decker plane to the bathroom, marvelling at what he kept saying. How *was* this building flying? I nudged him into the toilet and instructed him on what to do. I saw him fumble with his belt buckle and try to pull down his pants. I pulled at the mottled beige accordion doors and hoped he remembered how to relieve himself.

Periodically, I knocked. 'Dad, are you done?' I opened the door to peek in and saw the only father I'd ever really had made old and frail and thin from malnutrition. I didn't know that he had started wearing diapers and needed help removing them.

My mother's memory had returned, but not fully. At times, her language was still nonsensical. Those invisible friends or demons she had spoken to during my childhood were becoming a permanent fixture. When we arrived in Los Angeles, I drove us to their house. As we approached their driveway, I stopped and reached my hand out of the window to retrieve mail from their mailbox. My mother was beside me in the passenger seat, Mr Reyes behind. He must have been very confused, shifting from one environment to another.

I pulled the pile of advertisements and bills into the car, and quickly scanned through them to make sure I knew what needed to be paid. As I looked to the right, I saw that my mother understood—I was taking her belongings and asserting control over her domain. She began to scream and scratch at my arm, like a cat who suddenly snaps. She tried to claw her way back to omnipotence and retrieve her belongings. Her body was able. Her mind was not. I wondered—does agency belong to the able-bodied? Or to one with an able mind?

I quickly parsed out the mail, kept what was important and let my mother have the residual envelopes; I tucked the ones I needed under my seat. The skin that she had just clawed on my arms began to smart.

Not only did my mother want to control her belongings (and not only did she believe she was competent enough to manage her affairs), but she also still vehemently rejected mainstream medicine. The doctor in India told me that my mother needed to take anti-seizure pills to help heal her mind, otherwise the brain damage would become permanent. But my mother didn't think this needed to be followed.

I arranged for a court-appointed psychiatrist to evaluate her mental condition, as well as Mr Reyes's. The psychiatrist's assessment would grant me permanent conservatorship, and he would be able to testify as to whether my parents needed me to take control of their health as well.

The psychiatrist arrived only a few days after our arrival. As he assessed my parents, I paced around the backyard. I stopped to periodically look down at the ground, at the shadows of a palm tree and an elm. I could hear animals rustling through the bushes—snakes, rabbits and deer. It was the terrain I had hiked as a lonely child, when I ended up at Mr Reyes's house, and he always welcomed me in.

Questions haunted me as I waited: Am I doing the right thing? Is this selfish? Am I just getting back at my mother for abandoning me when I was only twelve years old?

I truly didn't know.

The psychiatrist came outside and approached me. 'Well,' he said, 'it's clear your mother is suffering from dementia from brain damage. Your father has Alzheimer's.'

He explained that if my mother took the medications required to heal her brain, she might recover, but for the time being, a conservatorship of her estate was necessary. He didn't believe my mother needed someone to control her health; she was ambulatory and seemingly able to take care of Mr Reyes. I told him that she would refuse care or medication, but he explained that the conservatorship of a person completely rips someone of their agency. The court would only approve if my parents were in a dire physical state. And at that time, it didn't seem as if they were.

My life without my parents was in disarray, too. Though I had got a string of elite postdocs, I could not find a job. I moved every two years and built a new life, Pablo and Devi still by my side. I chose toxic partners. I had fallen into an abusive relationship, one that mirrored my life with my mother.

I don't think I wanted responsibility of and control over my parents. The pressure made me feel like I couldn't breathe; there was a lump of air caught in my chest, and the stress of the demands being made hardened and compacted it into a boulder. The boulder kept threatening to move up my throat and choke me.

Although an unconscious part of me felt vindicated that I was the one to wield power, that power produced a kind of horror I had never been privy to, the kind that comes from realizing your parents are old and fragile and no longer able to care for themselves or you, even if they were never able to care for you to begin with.

One day, I was carrying the mail I had just retrieved to the wood-panelled guest unit of my parents' house. There was a pull-out sofa in front of me. My biological father's mahogany desk sat to my left, covered with the scratchings of my mother's financial history. I scanned the contents of the mail and removed the bills and bank statements, tucking them under my shirt so no one could see them. The soft edges of the envelopes tickled my abdomen; any bend of my body felt unnatural.

My mother was there, waiting for me. 'What are you doing?' she asked.

Her jaw was clenched as she began to shake. A baggy dress hung off her body like drapes. She had not washed her face, and a stubble of the rice and lentils I had made the night before dotted her lips. She reached out and grabbed the remaining mail. I had, once again, taken her belongings without asking, but this time I had legal permission.

With her mind not in her control, all she felt she had sovereignty over were her surroundings, her belongings. Control was something she needed, coveted and powerfully tried to acquire. As I grew older, she could not control me—and here I was, trying to rip away her authority.

Mr Reyes walked into the room. 'What is going on here?' he asked.

'She won't give me the bags!' my mother replied.

She understood the meaning of what was happening, but her mind couldn't provide the precise words. I imagined her brain—synapses searching for a definition, their short hands stretching out to find the right letters to assemble into the right words, then faltering, choosing 'bags' instead of 'envelopes'. Mr Reyes did not notice the mistake.

My mother looked through the mail. A large manila envelope from the Los Angeles County Court was in the stack. The law did not allow me to tuck this piece of mail under my shirt with the rest, though I wanted to. I didn't want my mother to know I was taking away her authority. But I had to tell her that she was being taken to trial; that, if she refused the conservatorship, she would get a court-appointed attorney and they would represent her in a fight against me.

She opened the envelope.

'You are taking us to the room!' she yelled. I knew what she really meant was court.

I tried to remain calm, to rationally explain, 'Ma, this is what is best for you. You can't remember to pay your bills. Someone needs to manage things. Wouldn't you rather it be me instead of a stranger? I'm just trying to help you.'

'No! No one is going to come into the house! No one!'

My mother's shaking was infectious. Mr Reyes began to shake, too. He didn't understand what I was saying, but he could feel my mother's fear and anger.

'There is nothing wrong with my head! Get out!' my mother yelled.

Mr Reyes joined her shrill notes. 'Yes, get out!'

'Fine,' I replied.

Somewhere, I knew my mother must not have completely meant to throw me out. But the rage she provoked in me felt unbearable and allowed me to succumb to her demand that I leave the house. Dealing with a person who would not see reality drove me past the point of sanity.

I walked past my parents, and my mother followed as I furiously pulled my clothes from hangers and shoved them into my suitcase. I rushed to my car, my mother still following me. Mr Reyes kept pace with her. I threw my suitcase into the trunk. It was one of the suitcases my mother and I had travelled with when I was a child, with a large red stripe of duct tape diagonally pasted across its face. I marvelled at how the tape had not fallen off even after twenty years. The tape was a talisman that had kept us safe during all our travels, even as everything else splintered.

As I drove away in my rental car, my mother stood in front of the garage, flailing about for comprehension. I gripped the steering wheel and searched the wide Pasadena roads, the exquisitely manicured lawns, the roses and bungalows, for somewhere to sleep.

The next day, I knew I'd have to return and take care of my mother.

26

MY MOTHER WAS NO LONGER just the mentally ill mother of my childhood. Now the beings that had always plagued her waltzed with dementia.

Friends and relatives didn't understand the conservatorship. Every day someone would call and yell, 'Why are you doing this to your mother!' I became a Cruella-type villain in my mother's story. Our roles were reversed. Over twenty years had passed since Mrs Gregory had confirmed that my mother's abandonment of me was real, that she was a bad mother. Now, I was a bad daughter.

With each phone call, I tried to remain calm and explain what a conservatorship was, how it was designed to take care of a vulnerable person in need of care. No one heard me.

With every accusation, I felt an assault on my insides. Each word was a small rat eating my brain, until I could no longer take it. I yelled back, 'I am not taking advantage of anyone! Why won't you understand that I am doing what is best for her?' Then, I would hang up.

It was mind-boggling that no one could see that my mother was sick; that Mr Reyes was sick. My mother did try and hide the voices, but other signs were there—the small things she couldn't recall—her inability to drive her car properly, for instance, which put her in physical danger; her failure to remember her own phone number; her obvious confusion of words and names; the ever-present threat of violence.

The only witness to my mother's violence had been Lilia, but I no longer kept in touch with her. And while no one believed my mother was becoming increasingly vulnerable, I knew that she was on a slippery slope—the brain aneurysm and her history of mental illness has caused sufficient damage.

I learned that with conservatorships, one could let an independent conservator take on the duty. But when they were hired, they had full control. Given the predicament I found myself in—my parents needed care, but I didn't wish to be in their presence—someone recommended an independent conservator; let's call her A. And she was granted a six-month hold on my parents until they were further assessed.

A. was a skinny woman in her fifties, with short, reddish hair. Diamonds sat on her pencil-thin fingers, and she always carried a designer Louis Vuitton doctor's purse that swung from her gold layered wrist. I'd call her repeatedly, unable to relinquish my desire to protect my parents, and when she wouldn't call me back, I'd worry as anxiously as a dog who is afraid of thunder.

In 2005, *The Los Angeles Times* uncovered how some independent conservators in LA County were misusing 'their near-parental power over fragile adults'.[3] They isolated their clients, overcharged until bills ran up to hundreds of thousands of dollars—and some clients rarely saw the light of day. While there wasn't much regulation around conservatorships at that time, the *Times* article did propel a change. The courts began to supervise with more scrutiny.

As it turned out, my lawyer furnished an astronomical bill. Under a conservatorship, the fees are paid by the conservatee's estate. I cannot describe the fear I felt watching these events unfold, even when I didn't want to deal with my parents myself.

Pushed to the wall, a few months after A.'s appointment, I decided to find a new lawyer, petition to be my parents' permanent conservator and remove A. from the role. I hired a probate attorney named John. He had a chiselled face, with a prim cadence to his speech. He was stringent in his practice, with an opinion on everything. I liked his strict attention to every detail of the law and the rules of the conservatorship. His fees were modest in comparison to the last attorney (although all legal fees are enormous). John fought the initial attorney's bill in court, and the judge approved our complaints, confirming my belief that I had been overcharged. With John by my side, I could not be seen as duping my mother—even if she believed I was; even if she told her friends I was taking advantage of her; even if people yelled at me and accused me of abusing her.

I had to look out for my mother, regardless of how it made my brain want to explode.

I sat in the LA County Court, waiting for a judge to arrive. A rectangular grid of fluorescent lights framed the ceiling. It was like being in the bowels of a Rubik's cube. The seal of California framed the judge's bench, perfectly centred. The courtroom itself was a cavern of wood panelling, patterned in russet-coloured rectangles. The witness box, the judge's bench, the four walls—all were brown, brown, more brown. Only the rows of chairs were a different colour, black and blue.

By coincidence, I was also in Los Angeles for the Modern Language Association (MLA) conference, where thousands of professors and graduate students, dressed in boring black suits, presented obscure papers, and scholars like me were interviewed for tenure-track jobs. The wealthier schools could afford hotel rooms where they assessed the interviewees. The less elite conducted their interviews at wooden tables spread across the banquet halls of the various Marriotts, Sheratons and Westins. I had a few interviews that year, but no job offers.

John and I met in the lobby of my hotel for coffee before the trial. The hotel was near the courthouse. He told me to dress conservatively, so that I would look 'presentable'. I tried to dress as I did to interview with schools like Dartmouth, Yale and Stanford.

Each time I interviewed for a job, I was told to be a wallflower, something I felt I couldn't possibly be. With a mother like mine, where could I have possibly learned to fit in like that? For each of the eight years I interviewed, I borrowed clothes from friends—boring suits that covered my extremities, my tattoos, anything and everything that made me stand out from the mass of black, brown and navy-blue outfits that patterned the conference halls. As a woman, and especially a woman of colour, I had to 'blend in' with the white men and women who populated the English departments at various elite universities. I had to tame and veil my sexuality. 'They won't hear what you are saying if you dress like you do,' I was told. I didn't question the systemic racism and sexism buried in these comments (until much later) because I wanted a job. I did whatever I needed to do so that the straight men who interviewed me didn't think I was desirable, and thus the women didn't think I was threatening.

That day, to feel accomplished, I wore a white button-up shirt with a collar that I had dry-cleaned at the hotel, as if the chemicals used to remove the shirt's impurities would wash my skin. I covered my shirt with a black blazer, large hook-and-eye closures securely fastening it against my chest. I donned a black pleated skirt, and covered my legs with black tights that were too hot for Los Angeles, even in January. I wore closed-toe shoes and not too much make-up—a hint of mascara, a slight caress of blush. I tied my hair neatly back into a bun, not a strand out of place, no bobby pins lacing my forehead.

As we drank cappuccinos from generic hotel cups, my lawyer told me, in the driest way, 'You look like you are going to a funeral.'

I laughed. 'Yeah, I guess I do.'

That day, I saw my mother for the first time since she had kicked me out of the house. Her shirt was shapeless, her pants printed in bold colours, as if a wide paintbrush dipped in primary colours had wiped itself all over her legs. Her hair was dyed with henna, so that her greys were red. All the ends remained jet-black. Her left eye still drooped, her eyelid almost covering her pupil. Her once symmetrical face appeared lopsided, but her skin was supple without many wrinkles, even though she was sixty-two. In comparison, my thirty-two years were beginning to show. Lines erupted from the corners of my eyes, and I had amassed large sunspots all over my face—melasma from years in the sun; years of trying to keep myself brown; years of emphasizing that I was Indian, a woman of colour, holding within me the history of a mentally ill Bengali immigrant mother. I looked more and more like my Dida, her skin decorated in brown spots. Shallow craters dug into my cheeks, the remnants of the times I had mutilated my face.

I walked into the courtroom with my lawyer, found our table and sat down. I wondered why the room was a perfect set of rectangles, if there was a meaning to the shape, if it somehow represented what the law tries to be—a set of orderly rules and boundaries, even if laws are always susceptible to change.

The judge looked over at me. I took in his grey and white handlebar moustache, so perfectly coiffed. His eyes moved back down to the documents before him. His glasses fell down to the bridge of his nose as he looked through the evidence. His hands shuffled through the papers. I could hear the click-click-click of the stenographer's keyboard. I looked at the security officer, who stood to the left of the judge's bench. My eyes fell on his gun. I had never touched a gun in my life; I imagined the guard lifting his weapon and aiming it directly at my heart, blood splattering all over my stiff white shirt.

The judge raised his head to look at me once more and pushed his glasses back up his nose. 'I see that your mother and father forgot to pay their mortgage and many of their bills. The house was in foreclosure?'

'Yes, Your Honour.'

My mother began to laugh the eerie laugh that reminded me of the day I had met my Tapati Mashi in the asylum, a laugh that indicated she was not completely within the realm of reason. She saw things as she wanted to see them, not as they were.

'No, no, no, no, no,' she said, as she kept laughing.

The judge looked over at her. I knew her cackle only bolstered my case.

Suddenly, I felt as if there were bricks on my chest. I raised my right arm and touched my heart. I felt the strength of those bricks inside of me. Taking control of a parent's life feels profoundly unnatural. They are supposed to be your guardians—you are not supposed to be theirs. I wondered once again if I was being vengeful by stripping away my mother's sovereignty; if I was getting back at her leaving me in India, when I'd felt the absolute loss of free will. I rumpled my forehead, wondering if I had it right, if my mother and Mr Reyes did need my help, if they could indeed take care of themselves. As I was thrown into the anomalous role of a parent, even though I doubted myself and my intentions, I stated the opposite.

'I don't believe that they can manage their affairs, Your Honour. My mother's memory has been affected by her aneurysm. My stepfather has Alzheimer's. They need my help.'

The judge nodded. 'There are other bills here that were not paid.'

'Yes, Your Honour.'

Suddenly, I recalled the judge who had examined my mother when I was eleven years old—much as this judge examined me now. I saw myself with my arm in a sling. I heard the judge interrogating my mother, asking if the settlement amount the woman offered was worth the cost of my arm. I recalled the paternalistic force of his tone. I felt my mother next to me trembling, as the judge scrutinized her. I suddenly understood the irony of the situation. Here I was, exactly two decades later, being judged on whether I had enough daughterly love to tend to my mother. I was on trial to determine my intentions, my competency, perhaps even my own grip on reality.

The tables had so perfectly turned.

Like many children, I had not thought of taking care of my ageing parents; how I might be asked to care for them even though they failed to care for me. How hard it can be to delight in the elderly! They are baby-like, but not babies. They don't have the fresh, supple flesh of a child; smooth, soft skin; big smiles and tiny clothes at which people marvel. Rather, they are viewed with dismay, and shunned and relegated to the confined rooms of nursing homes. My sympathy for my mother overwhelmed me. When the judge granted me conservatorship, neither my mother nor I knew what would happen to us, and I pined for an astrologer who could reveal our fate.

Some of my Indian friends believe that filial responsibility is unquestionable, deeply rooted in our psyches; a quantum law that cannot be seen. It. Just. Is.

I felt the duty of being an Indian daughter. And the lifelong pull towards my mother drew me in, the entanglement, regardless of time or space, contracting and expanding, once again.

But I was also an American.

The Indian/American struggle I had experienced my whole life manifested itself not in a story of assimilation, but in how I needed to care for my mother. In India, the role of the daughter is cultural; in the United States, litigiousness *is* our culture. I chose the 'Western' way. As with my 'plant marriage', even though I understood the cultural specificity of my mother's response, I made a choice. My mother was sick. She was vulnerable. And she was still unruly. To contend with her unruliness, I resolved to take the route of courts and lawyers. Perhaps I also chose the law because I needed to hire others to take over and keep myself at the safe distance from my family, protect my sanity, live in some borderland between Indian and American forms of caretaking.

In the end it didn't matter. Neither the East nor the West could save my mother.

WINTER 2015
DEPARTURE

DAY AFTER DAY, I SIT by my mother's side. I have refused her love for decades, flinched at her touch, recoiled from her embrace. She doesn't deserve my affection, that layer of warmth known as love. But as I sit by her side, and I am saturated in memories of our history, an unfamiliar love for her—a love I felt when I was a child but later tucked away in the dark corners of my subconscious—surfaces. Now that it's too late. I want to crawl into bed and curl up beside her. I want her small body to fit perfectly into all my nooks. I want to nuzzle up as we did when we were young and in love. I want to envelop her in my warmth. But there is no room for me in her bed and she is too frail to receive my embrace.

Instead, I lean in. Her fingers tremble and slowly inch towards me. I reach out and hold her hand. She shivers, and my touch and speech are all that I have to soothe her.

I find my voice. 'It's okay, Ma. I'm here.'

Her skin feels warm; her hands are wrinkled and have dried into a pattern of crisscrossed lines. As her fingers shake in my palm, I tighten my grip and sob.

The nurse, Roopa, scolds me in Bengali. 'Don't cry! Don't make her upset. It is bad for her health.'

My mother begins to weep in response. She moves her head ever so slightly, left to right—*no, no, no, no, no*. Then she turns her head to the wall beside her. She speaks to an unknown presence and growls.

In a hospital room in Kolkata, I find myself in the midst of a tragedy with all the pathos of a Greek myth. Here, lying before me, my mother is not an abstract theoretical text. I can hear our history in her attempts to speak. I read the wounds that spread across her body as the story of my family's disintegration. Her voice, only a whisper, speaks of the silence that surrounds mental illness in India. The sight of her reaching for me, taking my hand in hers, illuminates so many moments of our fierce attachment, our passionate break.

I squeeze her hand again. 'Don't cry,' I say. 'Everything is going to be okay.' Though I am not sure I believe my own words. '*Ami achi*. I'll take care of you.'

My mother tries to raise her head to meet my gaze. In a hushed voice, she murmurs, 'You're so pretty.'

I respond as I always do. 'Not as pretty as you, Ma.'

As I speak these words, I feel more love than I ever have felt, or as much as I must have felt when I was too young to remember.

As the days go by, my mother speaks to us in fragments, with obscure words. Sometimes she speaks to an unknown presence, but then she shifts back to the reality of me, of her nurses. For all the memories of strife with my mother, new memories form. My mother on a hospital bed with a wound that broke open her body; my mother crying from the suffering she has endured; my mother after a surgery that closed the gaping hole in her back; my mother made helpless and old. Her frailty and sickness sink us both into a space of rest, any lingering rage relinquished.

I spend a month with my mother and then place her in a rehabilitation home. Because my mother has inherited Mr Reyes's money, her estate, under the conservatorship, will pay all the bills. Once again, I will manage things from afar. Now, though, I don't want to be far away from my mother. It is the first time, since I was a young girl, that all I want is to be near her.

But I have to go back to Will and the life we have built, because I do miss him, but also because I have to find a job. Will needs my help to support our household.

The day I leave, I go to say goodbye and assure my mother that I will be back. I bring sweets to fatten her up. I hand-feed her and she slowly chews the soft, crumbly flesh of shondesh. I put a cloth to her mouth to remove the remnants, something she did for me when I was a baby, pictures of me with sticky mango checkered across my face, the pit in my palm, my mother smiling, a small rag in hand as she waits to clean me up—a moment where she was truly motherly.

'Ma, I will be back to take you home.'

'Yaaaaaaa,' she responds.

I hold this memory as I walk down the stairs. I stop on the second floor and push my back against the wall, scraping my body down to the ground. Gravity settles me.

I do not want to leave my mother. It is just like all the times I clung to her leg, pounded the floor and asked her not to leave me. Only now, once again, we are parted.

I shake from the force of this old emotion, and the awe and love that consumed me as a child, and let myself release a watershed of tears, somehow knowing that this is the last time I will ever see her. I know she will die in the place she was born, as she wants to.

27

I WAS SITTING ON THE marble steps of my new apartment building in Baltimore, Maryland, an old Greek revival brownstone with a red brick façade. It was three storeys high, the windows and edges moulded with cream cement. I didn't get any of the jobs I had interviewed for at the MLA that January, but I did receive a fellowship in the English department at Johns Hopkins University. Eight months had passed since the trial.

I had been living in Baltimore for two weeks, and there was an ease to my arrival, a feeling of being at home. It was a feeling I had not experienced since I was fifteen years during the final days of living in Kolkata, that dense city of beeping cars. Baltimore possessed the same gritty, dirty charm of Kolkata, only without the force of millions of bodies. The city's beat wasn't hard and loud as Kolkata's has been, but more of a slow thumping. Baltimore was a sleepy, ghostly town plagued with brutal policing and racial segregation, but still warm and charming, a strange mix of opposing forces. It was like Kolkata in that way, so poor, yet rich with art and culture. Both Kolkata and Baltimore had bad reputations. I identified with the place and was unafraid to be my flamboyant self—the woman I had lost when I had taught at Vassar.

My downstairs neighbour had invited me to hang out on the stoop with a bottle of red wine, two small mason jars, and a pack of Marlboro reds. We were smoking, drinking, talking, feeling the warmth of alcohol flowing through our veins and up to our heads. That's what people in Baltimore did—they 'stooped' it, watching people pass them by as they sat on the front steps of their buildings, talking to neighbours while drinking, and engaging in conversation to get to know each other.

My dogs, Pablo and Devi, had passed away a few months before my arrival; they died two weeks apart, and their deaths left me with a profound emptiness. I could not live without a dog in my home. Dogs had become the only form of family that felt safe. I felt clichéd in my attachment—I was that crazy dog lady destined to die alone in my apartment with two pets, who would eventually have to succumb to their most primitive needs and eat me. Regardless, I peered through websites, looking for a new dog to fill the silence. I wanted the pitter-patter of paws, the sharp shrillness of a Chihuahua bark, the clumps of hair from a little shedding beast. I found a small brown dog named Banjo. He had large bat ears that stuck out like antennae; they perked up when people walked by or when dogs urinated on the red fire hydrant or tree stump in front of my building.

While I sat on the stoop with Banjo, warm and alert on my lap, a big brown dog arrived to greet him. She shoved her large wet nose into Banjo's face, her fat tail wagging so hard her entire body moved with it. The man attached to this new dog had brown hair and light blue eyes that lit up his chiselled face. His broad shoulders looked strong and reassuring in a red and black flannel shirt. I drunkenly flirted with him for an hour, wondering if he was single, if he was someone who might want me, love me—or someone, like so many others, who would not. We began to see each other at the dog park. I went when I knew he would be there, and later found out that he did, too. We were almost too perfect, too cute, in our courtship. He was nervous during each run-in at the dog park, while I performed a level of confidence I did not possess. His name was Will.

We fell for each other with the ease I'd felt when I first arrived in Baltimore. Our sex was dirty and romantic. Will was not interminably ambivalent about me; he was securely sure. In turn, I was sure as well. He possessed an ability to love unconditionally, something he must have learned from the safety and security of a warm and loving home, a mother who wanted him, who never left him, with whom he did not fight. A mother who had proper boundaries—the mother that my mother was not.

I had no desire to have children. I didn't want that responsibility. We had been dating for four months. Because I was certain about him, I needed to know how he felt about kids.

'I don't really feel the need to biologically reproduce. It isn't like I've always wanted to be a father. It's not something I've really thought about,' Will responded when I told him my feelings about having children.

'I guess, if you ever feel like you want to have children, we can talk about adopting?' I said.

'I don't have a desire for anything right now, but if I do, we can talk about adopting. I don't know if bringing a child into this world is fair or ethical.' Will was always thinking about what was good and fair and ethical. It was one of the reasons I had fallen for him.

I didn't want children for the ethical reasons he outlined, but even more than that, I did not want to recreate the scenes of violence my mother and I had lived with, the violence my mother and Dida had quaked with. I imagined myself with a little girl, her baby-soft cheeks tanned by the glow of the sun. I pictured myself slathering sunscreen all over her skin, kissing her cheeks and brushing strands of hair off her face. I saw myself nestling her, warming her body on cold nights with cotton blankets. I imagined taking her to India, showing her the city of my childhood. But I also imagined violence born from a legacy of rage. A violence that I would be too weak to suppress when confronted by a little girl passing through the throes of puberty. I saw myself reaching for her ear and pulling-pushing her. I would worry about her every move, how her body would travel through an array of other bodies who wanted comfort and love and sustenance from her, who wanted that same sustenance that billions of people who roamed the planet wanted from the earth. When I thought of the fighting and strife building between me and my imaginary daughter, I recoiled. Would I pass on the illness that boiled in my family? I could not—I would not—reproduce.

I took care of my parents' affairs from afar while I built the life I had always wanted with Will. There aren't any words that adequately encapsulate what being loved and wanted feels like. Perhaps that is why we succumb to clichés when we describe 'true love' or 'the one'. As versed as I was in psychoanalysis and theory, I had no way to articulate what happened to me when I met Will, other than to say that I fell deeply, truly and utterly in love.

We moved in together after nine months. Our life took on a quotidian routine, but I was not bored. He came home every day after work and I cooked dinner. We frequently had people over on the weekends. Every night when we made love, I melted into his embrace. My body was a comma caught in his sentence, hooked into a life we'd designed, hoping the chapter we were writing would never end. The warmth I felt with him reminded me of the nights I spent as a child sleeping inside the curve of my mother's body, taking in the smell of her hair.

I still questioned my role as conservator and Will assured me, each day, that I was doing what was best for my parents. The accusations of abusing my mother continued. I had grown afraid of phone calls, for the caller was always my mother or a relative, someone who didn't understand what the conservatorship signified. My mother screamed into the phone and cried, begging me to give her back her money.

'I haven't taken anything,' I'd say. 'Every penny is spent for your care, Ma.'

I'd try to explain that the court made me do yearly accounting. I'd plead, 'Read the documents. They tell you everything, I promise.'

'You are lying!'

The phone calls were an infuriating loop.

I hired a team in California to do the work for me. A fiduciary managed the finances, and I tried to arrange for a person to go to my parents' house each day to check in on them. Mr Reyes needed full-time care, but my mother refused a nurse, and only allowed someone to stay with them when I threatened to call Adult Protective Services (APS).

I found out that my mother was making Mr Reyes wear dirty disposable diapers, laced with shit and urine. The reek of his incontinence was spreading across his home. Maria, a woman from the agency I had hired, knocked on their door each day. When Mr Reyes answered, he let her in. One day, Maria saw my mother at the kitchen sink, a disposable diaper in her hands, scrubbing the faeces out of the absorbent layers. Maria tried to take the diaper away from her, but my mother pushed her away, gripping the diaper between hands, now covered in Mr Reyes's waste. The agency Maria worked for called and told me that they would have to call APS if I did not do something. I wanted to drop everything and go, the way I had when I got the call about my mother's aneurysm. I wanted to remove Mr Reyes from my mother's care. But I was paralyzed. Both by the shock that the man I loved most was being so neglected, and terrified by the potential onslaught of my mother's rage.

The only recourse was to tell my mother that if the agency called APS, the state would take Mr Reyes away from her forever. She understood this much. If she didn't comply, she would be alone—even if she already was, because the Mr Reyes she had married no longer existed. My mother conceded, at last. She allowed us to place a caretaker in her home from nine to five. But no one was allowed to stay at night.

The phone rang one day, but this time it was not my mother or a relative; it was Sam, the man who ran the agency I had used to place a caretaker in my parents' home. Will and I were driving to our favourite restaurant in Baltimore. Will knew that any call from California was stressful for me, so he put his hand on my knee.

'Rani, your dad is being rushed to the hospital,' Sam told me.

'What happened?' I said, in panic, turning to Will.

'He had a fall last night and your mother left him there. The caregiver found him this morning covered in urine.'

I hung up the phone and told Will what had happened. Mr Reyes had fallen onto the chilly marble floor of the television room in the middle of November; he must have been so cold. My mother had possibly watched him fall, piss all over himself; maybe she had walked away because she was plagued by other demons. Maybe she felt unable to help.

I phoned my mother and asked her why she hadn't called for assistance, though I knew I would never receive an adequate answer.

'There is nothing wrong with him,' she said, laughing. 'These people are so silly.'

Mr Reyes's kidneys, it turned out, were failing; he was dying and needed hospice care. I placed him in a home, where he began to receive a morphine drip. I spoke with hospice advisors, but I did not fly to see him.

I should have, but a sense of immobility had taken over me, a fear of drowning in my mother's madness. I didn't want to confront all the accusations. I raised my hands to my hair and pulled. I wanted to hurt my body.

Will came and sat by me, gently removing my hands from my hair, just as I had done as a child when I found my mother speaking to someone I could not see. I will forever wonder if protecting my psyche was worth the cost of never seeing Mr Reyes again.

So many outside forces had determined my mother's life—my Dida's demands that she save the family with her beauty; the upheavals of history; my father's death; the men who used and abandoned her; her unruly child.

She *wanted* power over her life when there were monsters taking over her mind. She made up a story. A story where everything was fine.

But I know that I tell myself this to rationalize her irrationality. To maybe even excuse her neglect.

28

AMITAVA FIRST CALLED WHEN MR Reyes had been rushed to the hospital.

I had not heard about either him or Rekha for years. I had always felt warmth for Rekha and all the times she had tried to treat me like a normal teenage girl, showering me with gifts. The fact that it was Amitava who suddenly appeared, and not Rekha, was startling to me.

I assume my mother had, at some point, called Rekha and she handed the phone to Amitava. Or Rekha called my mother and Amitava found out about the conservatorship. Perhaps my mother reached out because she thought she needed a man to protect her, now that Mr Reyes's health was waning. My mother never really realized how much she *didn't* need a man, and how, in the final years of his life, Mr Reyes was no longer her partner or protector—he had become a stranger to us and to himself.

I was walking the dogs with Will. It was a cool, damp Baltimore winter day. The bare arms of dogwoods held up the sky. Our pups were smelling every tree stump with eager wet noses when the phone rang. I didn't recognize the number, but Mr Reyes was in the hospital, so I needed to answer every call.

'Rani, it's Amitava here. Where have you taken Mr Reyes? There is nothing wrong with him.' I could hear my mother in the background saying over and over again, 'Why did she take him away from me? He is fine ...'

At first, I tried to explain what had happened. 'You don't understand,' I said, 'he was left on the floor all night, his kidneys are failing, he needs to be in the hospital.' I thought perhaps my mother hadn't told Amitava the trajectory of events.

'He needs to be with his wife!' he responded.

'But she isn't in a position to take care of him,' I said, desperately hoping he would be on my side.

Amitava rejected the statement.

A few hours later, I received a call from Sam, who told me that Amitava and my mother were at the hospital, demanding Mr Reyes be released; that he had been kidnapped; that I was a terrible daughter. The hospital workers tried to explain that Mr Reyes was nearing death. Neither Amitava nor my mother believed so.

Today, I can tell that my mother—predisposed as she was to believe in passing astrologers—was deeply vulnerable. And her vulnerabilities were exacerbated by her dementia. Each time someone agreed with her, reiterated her belief that she wasn't sick, restated her position that I had taken control of her when all she wanted was to exert her free will, she was inclined to hold on to that person.

Even though three thousand miles of radio waves separated us, Amitava made me shake with fear whenever he called, until I finally stopped picking up the phone.

A few weeks later, the phone rang again. It was Sam, not Amitava. I knew this was the final call. At the other end, Sam held up the phone to Mr Reyes's ear so I could say my final words. I felt like punishing myself for not being with him in his final moment. Instead, I said: 'Dad, I am so sorry, I am so sorry about everything. I only wanted what's best. I love you.'

'I love you too, honey,' he whispered softly. I tried to hear his last breath, but I couldn't pin down the exact moment when he left the living.

I only had control of my mother's estate, so I did what was in my purview. I took care of the properties, paid the bills, gave my mother a stipend so she could shop for herself and continue to feel as if she had some autonomy. She was in mourning and called me, and this time I answered.

'Ma, are you okay?'

She said nothing. If I listened hard enough, I could hear the tears that fell from her eyes.

She asked someone I could not see or hear, 'Why?'

I felt pangs of empathy leap up and travel to the other end of the country. 'Ma, I am so, so sorry. I loved him, too.'

'Rani? Rani? There are gods following me,' she replied. 'There are so many, thousands and thousands, some very bad. I don't know what they want from me. What can I do?'

She told me that Amitava was 'The Boss', so she had to listen to him.

My jaw stiffened so tightly, I felt the sinewy pulse of my eardrums. It was the first time my mother had admitted she heard ghosts, described who they were, and articulated her afflictions. She had admitted Amitava had cast some kind of hold on her and had entered her psyche. I realized that this confession, tragic as it was, was also a moment of victory—she knew she was ill.

'Ma, I can get you some help. I can send someone to get you and take you to see a doctor. We can make sure no one hurts you.'

My mother's disclosure was fleeting.

'No! There is nothing wrong with me,' she retorted.

All I could do was hang up, trusting that the conservatorship would protect her. For while I was trying to do what was best for her, I had no way of making her do what was needed to save her life. I was beginning to see what an impossible task I'd taken on.

My mother's mind, darkness and all, was hers alone.

With conservatorships, court dates are scheduled to assess the fees charged by attorneys and any incidental fees charged by the conservator. Meticulous accounting needs to take place. When each court date arrived, Amitava appeared with a lawyer. He asked for my removal as my mother's conservator. My lawyer, John, defended me.

My mother believed Amitava had her best interests in mind. It hurt to think of it—while my life with my mother was defined by domestic conflict, I was still her daughter; Amitava was not kin. But then, children do take advantage of their parents, and elder abuse is astoundingly common. The National Council on Aging reports that one in ten people over sixty are subject to some form of elder abuse, and only one out of twenty-four report the abuse to authorities. Sixty per cent of abuse is perpetrated by family members. The judges and lawyers who questioned my intentions were right to do so.

During my time in the probate circuit, I learned just how many predatory people exist, waiting to find an elderly person near death to exploit; how these predators isolate the elderly, so they are the only ones who will take care of them; how they spin narratives of distrust. As the conservator of my mother's estate, I was able to make sure my mother was not exploited for financial gain. But I did not have conservatorship of her person. I could not prevent how she moved about the world.

I finished my postdoc at Hopkins and persisted in my desire for a job in academia. This desire led Will and me to Cambridge for a year of teaching at Harvard. Will and I got married four years into our relationship, and no one from my family attended our wedding. The women in my family, with their loud voices, had fallen away into an abyss of history from which they could not be recovered.

After a year of teaching at Harvard, I failed to find a subsequent job and decided to leave academia. I started waitressing at the bar I had worked at when I was twenty-one and getting my master's, a time when I believed I would flourish in academia. The transition was confusing. What was I qualified to do? I had no idea. A programme that would help me find my strengths outside academe seemed the only possibility.

My mother went alone to visit India. Amitava helped her get on the plane. I didn't think he knew who was waiting on the other side—Rima Mashi. I imagined my mother's confusion and instability, how she moved in and out of reality. Did she speak to ether while thousands of miles in the air? Did she get lost in the airport in Dubai? Did she laugh at the pretty stewardesses in their bright red lipstick?

Amitava continued to go to every accounting in court. I left the business of handling him and my mother's estate to the experts—the hired fiduciaries and lawyers—and concentrated on my life with Will and our three rescue dogs.

Until I received the message: *You need to bring your mother back home.*

WINTER 2016
ENDINGS

I DREAM OF MY MOTHER. She is in the pink sweater that I found her in when I arrived in India two months ago. It is unbuttoned and no longer stifling her. She is falling into an abyss, her arms stretched out towards me. Wisps of her gold and grey hair crisscross her face. I reach out my hand and try to catch hold of her, but she slips away from me. I hear her voice, a whisper, *Rani, save me*. I wake up.

It is March, a new year has arrived. The damp, cold air of the late Cambridge winter slips through our bedroom window. The slender breeze overwhelms the dry warmth emanating from the baseboard heaters and spills over to the bed. The draught makes me shiver.

Will sleeps soundly beside me. Pancake and Banjo are curled up between us. I look over at my phone, it is 6 a.m. There are missed calls from Ritwik and Kabita and a WhatsApp message that reads: *She's gone*.

I break in two.

I fly to Kolkata that night by myself. Ritwik and Kabita are waiting for me. They have arranged everything—a hearse to pick up my mother as soon as I land; a trip to the crematorium; a priest to perform shraddha; a rental car to take me to the US consulate to wait in line and get the final document that proves my mother really is dead.

I am determined to follow the Hindu rituals Kabita details for me. I want to abide by the rules, respect my mother in the precise ways that she would have desired. I do not mock the observance the way I did when I married the plant. Although mourning obscures actions and events, I try hard to pay attention to every instruction. I haven't eaten meat. I haven't bathed since I received the message my mother was dead. I wear white on the plane. I do not once question my submission.

It seems natural to perform, with veneration, all the rituals my mother had believed in. How else might I prove my love for her—as if all those trips to save her haven't been enough? Because, for me, they are not. I cannot imagine a time when I will not feel guilt that I did not visit her earlier, that I did not prevent the months of torture she endured, that I was too busy protecting my psyche from her rage. That I did everything too late. That I was a terrible daughter.

I reach out to hug Kabita and Ritwik. Kabita was the emergency contact for my mother. She and Ritwik were at the hospital when my mother was declared dead. They quietly listened while doctors told them my mother had died from internal bleeding—a possible undetected ulcer. This happens, the doctors said. She had been so very weak, her body was so broken, they were unable to stop the bleeding.

My mother is now the unliving. Will her death allow me to comprehend our story? Does hindsight really make things clear?

My understanding of my mother has always arrived through the books I consumed; through accounts that told me that the history of colonial rule and witnessing physical trauma mutated into tortured minds. Now, my mother's mind is no longer tortured, and I want to honour her death.

We get to the hospital and a hearse arrives, so unlike the hearses used for funerals in the United States, with their tinted windows that shroud the casket and provide anonymity to the corpse. This hearse has clear windows and lights that will illuminate my mother's body as we travel to the crematorium, a place I've never been.

Two men at the hospital lead me to a row of drawers, almost hidden, blending into the building's outer concrete wall. The men pull my mother out of a small, refrigerated hole—a tiny space for her tiny body. I look away. My finger lingers on the dusty surface of the hearse—a tactile reminder that I am still alive, on Earth, touching, feeling, breathing. When I look back, her body is on the ground. There are cotton balls in her nose. Her knees are still bent as they were when I last saw her. Her body has shrivelled into a prune. Her mouth is concave because her dentures have been removed. My knees begin to crash into the ground, but Ritwik catches me.

Kabita gently covers my mother in a white sari. Men who work for the hospital lay tuberoses, garlands and wreaths all over her, as well as those tiny white flowers that smell so sweet—rajnigandha. They mask the smell of a deteriorating corpse. The men hand me a wreath. I walk towards my mother's body and kneel to place it upon her.

The men pick my mother up and put her in the hearse, her body now incandescent because of the florescent lights. I watch them drive away, while young boys hang on the windows of the hearse, throwing khoi and yelling: *Bolo Hori, Hori Bol!* We follow them.

The crematorium is an assemblage of buildings. In one, you get an Indian death certificate. In another, there is a waiting room. In yet another, two furnaces, so two bodies can burn at the same time. On the dirt floor where the dead wait, mourners perform the rituals in preparation for the corpses that will soon become ash. We are second in line; other mourners form behind us. We carry my mother and put her next to a dead woman, newly deceased and older than her; her skin still glowing with life. The three days my mother spent in the refrigerator have chilled her corpse and now she is melting. I kneel beside her, waiting for a priest to arrive to perform last rites. I take part of the white sari Kabita has laid upon her and wipe her face. I keep dabbing her skin to soak up the condensation, but the droplets of moisture stubbornly reproduce themselves. I stop and move down to touch her feet, which are stiff. I grip her legs and move my hands up her corpse, feeling her weight, her flesh, her limbs, while she is still whole. I hold her tightly, very tightly, as if I am trying to awaken her, as if I believe my touch is magic and suddenly, she will come alive. My hands reach her forehead and I move my fingers through her hair. This hair was once a thick black blanket that I nuzzled my face into at night, hair that she cut to be an American, hair that she laced with bobby pins to hide the bald patches, hair that hung from her heart-shaped face and accentuated her diagonal cheeks, her arched eyebrows and large eyes, hair that reminded me that she was my mother, despite her aching mind. I touch the few remaining silver and gold strands and the devotion I had for her as a child saturates me. I no longer care about her fits of rage, the voices that haunted her or that ugliness that gripped her when she was possessed by demons. My mother was haunted by centuries of unrest. The forces of history forged who she was and how she cared for me. The disgrace of Tapati Mashi's madness prevented her from seeking help.

Mental illness is stigmatized everywhere. Those who are mad are hidden. When we confront lost minds on streets, we look away and feel frightened. We want to forget that mentally ill people exist. We deny that every one of us can come undone by grief or trauma, by the constraints society puts on us. Instead, we demonize those whose minds churn, lock them up, shudder when we hear their rattling tongues. In the United States, the stigma varies across the many communities that make up the nation, based on class, ethnicity and race. But the unconscious burden of colonialism brings another layer to the perception and denial of mental afflictions. When I think of colonized people—denigrated for centuries because of their beliefs, their skin, their religion, and viewed by white men and women as irrational and crude—I think of the Calibans and Bertha Masons of the world who had to be tamed and brought to salvation by white powers, but I think also of my own Tapati Mashi. I think of how frightened I was of her as a child and how she embodied the things that colonial powers deemed her to be.

As a scholar, I tried making sense my family's compromises and negotiations as a result of these wounds—my Dida's marriage at age twelve; how she bore eight children, their suckling mouths, their demanding hands pulling at her until she'd shrivelled in size; her life in poverty because her husband, my Dadu, wanted to escape. My Tapati Mashi, widowed at eighteen during a time when this meant she had no future. My mother, a witness to the violence my Dadu had inflicted upon Tapati Mashi and subject to my Dida's colonized mind. My mother, who would eventually become a widow too. My own story with my mother was an extension of these histories, a story as simple as the struggle between love and hate. For, how do you describe the pull of a ferocious mother? I don't have an answer to the question. All I know is that I must honour her.

A priest comes up to us and hands me three, four, five incense sticks. He lights them, or I light them—I don't know. The priest tells me to walk around my mother's body three times as he reads passages in Sanskrit. He asks me to recite the words along with him, words I cannot pronounce. I feel inauthentic—not Indian. American. But this ritual is not about me; this is about my mother. The priest draws my hands over to a bowl of holy water and tells me to pour some into her mouth. Burning incense must follow. *Mukher agun*—fire to the mouth. Tiny bits of ash stick to her lips. I want to wipe them off so she can breathe. I feed her small bits of rice. I cannot register the order of the ritual because, all at once, I am not truly there. My mind has ventured elsewhere to protect me from my grief. More men arrive, and I help them lift my mother and place her on an iron bed. They pull a handle, a gate opens, and I see the tunnel of flames. The men push her in. I watch her pale grey face one last time, her pink sweater. And then the blaze devours her. They close the gates, and my mother is gone.

We wait for her to burn. After an hour has passed, Ritwik and I descend to the basement of the crematorium to gather my mother's remains. Smoke from the burned bodies and ash is all around us. I encounter a heap of bones of different shapes and sizes, a mound that stands taller than me, remnants of all the humans who have died that night, that day. I stop, stare and wonder: how many people are blended into that mountain of skeleton and cinders? How many lives churn into one? Does the mixture of their bones mean their histories intertwine? A man who worked at a bank now lives with a mother of three; a young girl who died too soon is embraced by a grandmother who died when it was 'appropriate'.

I don't smell anything. I don't know if the ash from burnt bodies travels to my nose and tickles it, if I am inhaling the dust of lost lives, if my eyes smart from the remnants of bodies still burning. I lose my sensory recollection as I move towards a container that resembles a coal scuttle, as if this dungeon-like space is a coal mine and bodies are being burned for energy.

A man points to the metal cauldron and tells me it contains my mother. I expect ash, the consistency of baby powder, the texture of the vibhuti Sai Baba produced from his hands—

something holy. Instead, I see bones that are still burning. A white powder forms a film atop the neon orange. The man pours water from the Ganga to quell the heat. *Are they really hers?* I think. Or is the scuttle filled with a mélange of bones from bodies that burned before her? The man, I learn later, is not accustomed to giving ashes to a mourner. We are not supposed to be in the basement. At the crematorium, bodies are not pulverized and given to loved ones who want to keep or scatter the remains. We are supposed to wait upstairs until I am given my mother's navel, which I will throw into the Ganga.

Ritwik reaches out his small hands, places them into the cauldron, and picks up my mother's bones, which, despite the holy water, still sizzle. He places them in a clear plastic container. I want to sprinkle a bit of her ashes in the Ganga, carry the rest to California, where I will give them a home, maybe take some to London, place a part of her in each of the places she once called home, a transnational scattering of her ashes, a lingering map of her existence.

Then the man hands me her umbilicus, still warm and wrapped in terracotta. I am told the belly button doesn't burn the way the rest of the body does. It remains impenetrable. The men at the crematorium wrap it in thick, wet clay, so I can carry it to the Ganga and throw it in.

We travel to the river, my mother's navel wrapped in clay sitting in my hands. I cradle the site of our attachment, my original home. As I walk to the water, I watch stick figures along the bank mimic my movements, a shadow of all the people who have lost someone. Do their stories possess the same elements as mine—madness, colonialism, colourism, the gendered constraints on women, tormented generations of mothers and daughters shattering each other's lives, as a mother abandons a daughter, as a sister tortures her kin, as a father pummels his daughter in the hope that he can beat her madness out of her?

I raise my hand to throw my mother into the sacred river. Her navel arcs across the midnight sky, then begins its descent into peace.

Nothing could give my mother deliverance but her death.

I am the last remaining part of my mother. If my belly button is thrown into the Ganga when I die, it will not be a daughter who performs the ritual. No child will live to tell of my existence. This book is the body through which my mother and my story will carry on.

Suddenly, I miss the mother that my mother was not, and the mother my mother always was.

ACKNOWLEDGEMENTS

THERE ARE MORE PEOPLE TO thank than I can remember, both in terms of the events in this story, and the encouragement and advice writing it.

Writing is never a solitary process, even if it appears that it is. I want to give gratitude to the many people from all the places I have lived, people who helped me in the various stages of this difficult tale, and the arduous process of writing it.

To Jigna Desai: you have been an older sister, championing my writing and career from so early on, reading every sentence I have ever written, seeing my worth when no one else did.

To Vernadette Vicuña Gonzalez: thank you for reviewing my work, new and old, and supporting each of my literary endeavours.

To Simon Han, for your comments and advice at the end stages of editing the manuscript and for teaching me the ways of fiction writing as I continue my career.

To my friends at Harvard, Linda Schlossberg, Caroline Light and Krishna Lewis: your support has been invaluable.

To my classmates and teachers at Grub Street and the Fine Arts Work Center, who helped me through the process of writing the first draft. Alex Marzano Lesnevich, Michelle Seaton, Garrard Conley, Wendy C. Ortiz and Joan Wickersham: you all shepherded me through my infant stages as a writer.

Thank you to the Massachusetts Cultural Council for awarding me a fellowship to finish this book.

To Patrick Watson and George Rogers, for offering me a place by the sea to write every summer.

To the friends who, throughout my nine years of writing, read drafts: Tara, Joanna, Liz, Josh, Heather, Caroline, Chris, Anmol and Susan Baily, Aaron.

To Mercy Romero, Chris Roebuck and Heather Butler, for over a decade spent talking about the pain and joy of being a writer.

To Susan Stryker, rockstar historian, for consistently backing me and my work.

Thank you to the many members of the Boston writing community, who have helped me in finding an agent and cultivating my career.

To Katrin Schumann: you have been such a wonderful friend and fellow writer, showing me how to navigate what can feel like a treacherous landscape called the literary marketplace.

Thank you, Steve and Audrey Bennett, for the beautiful website you made to help me market my work.

Thank you Ananya Vajpeyi: for your encouragement and for helping me find an agent in India.

To my former students, Sasanka Jinadasa and Nu Xiong: it has been amazing having you both in my life and sharing my writing with you over the last thirteen years. Your belief in me as a teacher and artist has been the kind of experience that keeps my love for teaching alive. Leann Peterson and Jason Wu: for being there for me during an extremely difficult time. And to all my students, especially my Asian American students: I wrote this story in part for you, to break the silence around mental illness within our disparate communities.

To Dr Moses and your psychic aide in finding a name for my afflictions, for helping to steady me when I was at my unruliest.

To Ocean Vuong, Marjan Kamali and Viet Thanh Nguyen for your wonderful words.

Eileen Pollack: thank you for helping me edit earlier versions of the book and for teaching me to hone my writing.

To Elana Seplow-Jolley: you are a master editor. Without you, this book would have never found its shape. I treasure working with you. You are my book therapist.

To my cousin Niraj Singh: as annoying as you are, you are family. ☺

Poppy and Krishna Mashi: thank you for believing in me and sharing your stories.

I want to also thank Anna Newheiser: I earnestly appreciate the time you spent helping me take care of my parents in Los Angeles. It was so much work, and you were there with me.

Annu Jalais, for travelling with me.

Tami: you supported me when I really needed it, and you didn't have to.

To Kasturi: your assistance at the tail end of this story was crucial. I could not have accomplished any of it without you. I am truly indebted.

To my legal team, J. Gorton, Daniel Herbert, Kirsten A. Brown, for your commitment to my case.

To Sumana Ghosh: you were the first person to show me the bond of friendship. And thank you to your mother, Shanta, for her generosity.

Kingshook Biswas and Devashish Ray: I appreciate the kindness and care you showed my mother as she laid in the nursing home, waiting for me to bring her home.

To Abhik Sarkar, for reading my writing and spending time with me as a young girl, sitting on the steps of the Kolkata Metro, talking for hours.

Susmit Biswas: your incalculable help was vital. I know I did not always appear to appreciate the things you did to save me and my mother, but rest assured, I feel it as an essential part of who I am, as if without you, I would not exist.

Kabita Lindenmeyer: you are the mother I always wanted. I hope the narration of your role in this story comes close to illustrating all the things you did for me and my mother.

To Eliza Childs, for your constant reassurance.

Sau-ling Wong: you are a wonderful mentor, so rare. For over twenty years, you have cheered on my career and writing. Thank you.

My agent in the United States, Lucy Cleland: thank you for taking a chance on this book and me *and* your patience for your most anxious client.

To Naomi Barton and A Suitable Agency: for your passion and commitment to the project.

Dharini Bhaskar: I am in awe of how much you love this text. I am so grateful. Thank you for giving it a home.

To my former pups, Devi and Pablo: you saved me over and over again. I hope you are with each other in doggie heaven, jumping over rainbows.

To Mr Reyes: how astonishing that I could have found a wonderful father so much later in life. You loved me as if I were your own and I adored your warm embrace, your kind words, your loyalty to my mother, even when she was painfully difficult.

To William Prescott Melton: never did I think I would find someone so utterly unambivalent about me. You have given me the unconditional love I never had. I love you more than you know, and I hope our story, with our generations of furry children, never ends. Banjo and Poppy, thank you for introducing us. Poppy you are the friendliest dog in the world. Banjo, you were my little strange bundle of a pup who could sing *I love you* and grumble like a revving engine. You are so missed. Pancake, up in the sky, you were a hellion of loveable proportions. Martini and Samosa: you are our silly little neurotic monsters—we love you all.

And finally, to my mother. My love will forever be entangled with you across time and space. Now that you are gone, how will I ever know who I am?

NOTES

1. Amitav Ghosh, *The Shadow Lines* (New Delhi: Penguin, 2009).
2. Ashis Nandy, *The Intimate Enemy: Loss and Recovery of Self under Colonialism* (New Delhi: Oxford University Press, 2009).
3. Robin Fields, Evelyn Larrubia and Jack Leonard, 'When a Family Matter Turns into a Business', *The Los Angeles Times*, in <https://www.latimes.com/local/la-me-conserve13nov13-story.html>, 13 November 2005.

ABOUT THE AUTHOR

Rani Neutill is a recipient of the 2022 Artist Fellowship from the Massachusetts Cultural Council. She has taught ethnic American and postcolonial literature at Harvard, Yale, Johns Hopkins University and other institutions, and is presently teaching writing and Asian American literature at Emerson College and Tufts University. Rani has co-edited *Bangtan Remixed: A Critical BTS Reader* (Duke University Press). Her work has appeared in *The New York Times Book Review*, *Al Jazeera English*, CNN, *The Washington Post*, *Longreads, The Rumpus*, amongst other publications. She lives in Cambridge, MA, with her partner.

HarperCollins *Publishers* India

At HarperCollins India, we believe in telling the best stories and finding the widest readership for our books in every format possible. We started publishing in 1992; a great deal has changed since then, but what has remained constant is the passion with which our authors write their books, the love with which readers receive them, and the sheer joy and excitement that we as publishers feel in being a part of the publishing process.

Over the years, we've had the pleasure of publishing some of the finest writing from the subcontinent and around the world, including several award-winning titles and some of the biggest bestsellers in India's publishing history. But nothing has meant more to us than the fact that millions of people have read the books we published, and that somewhere, a book of ours might have made a difference.

As we look to the future, we go back to that one word—a word which has been a driving force for us all these years.

Read.

Harper Collins · 4th · HARPER FICTION · HARPER NON-FICTION · HARPER BUSINESS · HCCB HARPERCOLLINS CHILDREN'S BOOKS

HARPER DESIGN · Harper Sport · HARPER PERENNIAL · HARPER VANTAGE · हार्पर हिन्दी · BOOKTOPUS